# This planner belongs to:

_______________

# 2025

## January

| S | M | T | W | T | F | S |
| --- | --- | --- | --- | --- | --- | --- |
|  |  |  | 1 | 2 | 3 | 4 |
| 5 | 6 | 7 | 8 | 9 | 10 | 11 |
| 12 | 13 | 14 | 15 | 16 | 17 | 18 |
| 19 | 20 | 21 | 22 | 23 | 24 | 25 |
| 26 | 27 | 28 | 29 | 30 | 31 |  |

## February

| S | M | T | W | T | F | S |
| --- | --- | --- | --- | --- | --- | --- |
|  |  |  |  |  |  | 1 |
| 2 | 3 | 4 | 5 | 6 | 7 | 8 |
| 9 | 10 | 11 | 12 | 13 | 14 | 15 |
| 16 | 17 | 18 | 19 | 20 | 21 | 22 |
| 23 | 24 | 25 | 26 | 27 | 28 |  |

## March

| S | M | T | W | T | F | S |
| --- | --- | --- | --- | --- | --- | --- |
|  |  |  |  |  |  | 1 |
| 2 | 3 | 4 | 5 | 6 | 7 | 8 |
| 9 | 10 | 11 | 12 | 13 | 14 | 15 |
| 16 | 17 | 18 | 19 | 20 | 21 | 22 |
| 23 | 24 | 25 | 26 | 27 | 28 | 29 |
| 30 | 31 |  |  |  |  |  |

## April

| S | M | T | W | T | F | S |
| --- | --- | --- | --- | --- | --- | --- |
|  |  | 1 | 2 | 3 | 4 | 5 |
| 6 | 7 | 8 | 9 | 10 | 11 | 12 |
| 13 | 14 | 15 | 16 | 17 | 18 | 19 |
| 20 | 21 | 22 | 23 | 24 | 25 | 26 |
| 27 | 28 | 29 | 30 |  |  |  |

## May

| S | M | T | W | T | F | S |
| --- | --- | --- | --- | --- | --- | --- |
|  |  |  |  | 1 | 2 | 3 |
| 4 | 5 | 6 | 7 | 8 | 9 | 10 |
| 11 | 12 | 13 | 14 | 15 | 16 | 17 |
| 18 | 19 | 20 | 21 | 22 | 23 | 24 |
| 25 | 26 | 27 | 28 | 29 | 30 | 31 |

## June

| S | M | T | W | T | F | S |
| --- | --- | --- | --- | --- | --- | --- |
| 1 | 2 | 3 | 4 | 5 | 6 | 7 |
| 8 | 9 | 10 | 11 | 12 | 13 | 14 |
| 15 | 16 | 17 | 18 | 19 | 20 | 21 |
| 22 | 23 | 24 | 25 | 26 | 27 | 28 |
| 29 | 30 |  |  |  |  |  |

## July

| S | M | T | W | T | F | S |
| --- | --- | --- | --- | --- | --- | --- |
|  |  | 1 | 2 | 3 | 4 | 5 |
| 6 | 7 | 8 | 9 | 10 | 11 | 12 |
| 13 | 14 | 15 | 16 | 17 | 18 | 19 |
| 20 | 21 | 22 | 23 | 24 | 25 | 26 |
| 27 | 28 | 29 | 30 | 31 |  |  |

## August

| S | M | T | W | T | F | S |
| --- | --- | --- | --- | --- | --- | --- |
|  |  |  |  |  | 1 | 2 |
| 3 | 4 | 5 | 6 | 7 | 8 | 9 |
| 10 | 11 | 12 | 13 | 14 | 15 | 16 |
| 17 | 18 | 19 | 20 | 21 | 22 | 23 |
| 24 | 25 | 26 | 27 | 28 | 29 | 30 |
| 31 |  |  |  |  |  |  |

## September

| S | M | T | W | T | F | S |
| --- | --- | --- | --- | --- | --- | --- |
|  | 1 | 2 | 3 | 4 | 5 | 6 |
| 7 | 8 | 9 | 10 | 11 | 12 | 13 |
| 14 | 15 | 16 | 17 | 18 | 19 | 20 |
| 21 | 22 | 23 | 24 | 25 | 26 | 27 |
| 28 | 29 | 30 |  |  |  |  |

## October

| S | M | T | W | T | F | S |
| --- | --- | --- | --- | --- | --- | --- |
|  |  |  | 1 | 2 | 3 | 4 |
| 5 | 6 | 7 | 8 | 9 | 10 | 11 |
| 12 | 13 | 14 | 15 | 16 | 17 | 18 |
| 19 | 20 | 21 | 22 | 23 | 24 | 25 |
| 26 | 27 | 28 | 29 | 30 | 31 |  |

## November

| S | M | T | W | T | F | S |
| --- | --- | --- | --- | --- | --- | --- |
|  |  |  |  |  |  | 1 |
| 2 | 3 | 4 | 5 | 6 | 7 | 8 |
| 9 | 10 | 11 | 12 | 13 | 14 | 15 |
| 16 | 17 | 18 | 19 | 20 | 21 | 22 |
| 23 | 24 | 25 | 26 | 27 | 28 | 29 |
| 30 |  |  |  |  |  |  |

## December

| S | M | T | W | T | F | S |
| --- | --- | --- | --- | --- | --- | --- |
|  | 1 | 2 | 3 | 4 | 5 | 6 |
| 7 | 8 | 9 | 10 | 11 | 12 | 13 |
| 14 | 15 | 16 | 17 | 18 | 19 | 20 |
| 21 | 22 | 23 | 24 | 25 | 26 | 27 |
| 28 | 29 | 30 | 31 |  |  |  |

# Year in Pixels

| | J | F | M | A | M | J | J | A | S | O | N | D |
|---|---|---|---|---|---|---|---|---|---|---|---|---|
| 1. | | | | | | | | | | | | |
| 2. | | | | | | | | | | | | |
| 3. | | | | | | | | | | | | |
| 4. | | | | | | | | | | | | |
| 5. | | | | | | | | | | | | |
| 6. | | | | | | | | | | | | |
| 7. | | | | | | | | | | | | |
| 8. | | | | | | | | | | | | |
| 9. | | | | | | | | | | | | |
| 10. | | | | | | | | | | | | |
| 11. | | | | | | | | | | | | |
| 12. | | | | | | | | | | | | |
| 13. | | | | | | | | | | | | |
| 14. | | | | | | | | | | | | |
| 15. | | | | | | | | | | | | |
| 16. | | | | | | | | | | | | |
| 17. | | | | | | | | | | | | |
| 18. | | | | | | | | | | | | |
| 19. | | | | | | | | | | | | |
| 20. | | | | | | | | | | | | |
| 21. | | | | | | | | | | | | |
| 22. | | | | | | | | | | | | |
| 23. | | | | | | | | | | | | |
| 24. | | | | | | | | | | | | |
| 25. | | | | | | | | | | | | |
| 26. | | | | | | | | | | | | |
| 27. | | | | | | | | | | | | |
| 28. | | | | | | | | | | | | |
| 29. | | | | | | | | | | | | |
| 30. | | | | | | | | | | | | |
| 31. | | | | | | | | | | | | |

## Color Codes

## Notes

# January 2025

| MONDAY | TUESDAY | WEDNESDAY | THURSDAY |
|---|---|---|---|
|  |  | 1 | 2 |
| 6 | 7 | 8 | 9 |
| 13 | 14 | 15 | 16 |
| 20 | 21 | 22 | 23 |
| 27 | 28 | 29 | 30 |

# January 2025

| FRIDAY | SATURDAY | SUNDAY | NOTES |
|---|---|---|---|
| 3 | 4 | 5 | ○ |
| | | | ○ |
| | | | ○ |
| | | | ○ |
| | | | ○ |
| 10 | 11 | 12 | ○ |
| | | | ○ |
| | | | ○ |
| | | | ○ |
| 17 | 18 | 19 | ○ |
| | | | ○ |
| | | | ○ |
| | | | ○ |
| | | | ○ |
| 24 | 25 | 26 | ○ |
| | | | ○ |
| | | | ○ |
| | | | ○ |
| | | | ○ |
| 31 | | | NOTES |

# February 2025

| MONDAY | TUESDAY | WEDNESDAY | THURSDAY |
|---|---|---|---|
|  |  |  |  |
| 3 | 4 | 5 | 6 |
| 10 | 11 | 12 | 13 |
| 17 | 18 | 19 | 20 |
| 24 | 25 | 26 | 27 |

# February 2025

| FRIDAY | SATURDAY | SUNDAY | NOTES |
|---|---|---|---|
|  | 1 | 2 | ○ |
|  |  |  | ○ |
|  |  |  | ○ |
|  |  |  | ○ |
|  |  |  | ○ |
| 7 | 8 | 9 | ○ |
|  |  |  | ○ |
|  |  |  | ○ |
|  |  |  | ○ |
| 14 | 15 | 16 | ○ |
|  |  |  | ○ |
|  |  |  | ○ |
|  |  |  | ○ |
|  |  |  | ○ |
| 21 | 22 | 23 | ○ |
|  |  |  | ○ |
|  |  |  | ○ |
|  |  |  | ○ |
|  |  |  | ○ |
| 28 |  |  | NOTES |

| MONDAY | TUESDAY | WEDNESDAY | THURSDAY |
|---|---|---|---|
|  |  | 1 | 2 |
| 6 | 7 | 8 | 9 |
| 13 | 14 | 15 | 16 |
| 20 | 21 | 22 | 23 |
| 27 | 28 | 29 | 30 |

| FRIDAY | SATURDAY | SUNDAY | NOTES |
|---|---|---|---|
| 3 | 4 | 5 | ○ |
| | | | ○ |
| | | | ○ |
| | | | ○ |
| | | | ○ |
| 10 | 11 | 12 | ○ |
| | | | ○ |
| | | | ○ |
| | | | ○ |
| 17 | 18 | 19 | ○ |
| | | | ○ |
| | | | ○ |
| | | | ○ |
| | | | ○ |
| 24 | 25 | 26 | ○ |
| | | | ○ |
| | | | ○ |
| | | | ○ |
| | | | ○ |
| 31 | | | NOTES |

# April 2025

| MONDAY | TUESDAY | WEDNESDAY | THURSDAY |
| --- | --- | --- | --- |
|  | 1 | 2 | 3 |
| 7 | 8 | 9 | 10 |
| 14 | 15 | 16 | 17 |
| 21 | 22 | 23 | 24 |
| 28 | 29 | 30 |  |

# April 2025

| FRIDAY | SATURDAY | SUNDAY | NOTES |
|---|---|---|---|
| 4 | 5 | 6 | ○ |
| | | | ○ |
| | | | ○ |
| | | | ○ |
| | | | ○ |
| 11 | 12 | 13 | ○ |
| | | | ○ |
| | | | ○ |
| | | | ○ |
| 18 | 19 | 20 | ○ |
| | | | ○ |
| | | | ○ |
| | | | ○ |
| | | | ○ |
| 25 | 26 | 27 | ○ |
| | | | ○ |
| | | | ○ |
| | | | ○ |
| | | | ○ |
| | | | **NOTES** |

# May 2025

| MONDAY | TUESDAY | WEDNESDAY | THURSDAY |
|---|---|---|---|
|  |  |  | 1 |
| 5 | 6 | 7 | 8 |
| 12 | 13 | 14 | 15 |
| 19 | 20 | 21 | 22 |
| 26 | 27 | 28 | 29 |

# May 2025

| FRIDAY | SATURDAY | SUNDAY | NOTES |
|---|---|---|---|
| 2 | 3 | 4 | |
| 9 | 10 | 11 | |
| 16 | 17 | 18 | |
| 23 | 24 | 25 | |
| 30 | 31 | | NOTES |

# June 2025

| MONDAY | TUESDAY | WEDNESDAY | THURSDAY |
|---|---|---|---|
|  |  |  |  |
| 2 | 3 | 4 | 5 |
| 9 | 10 | 11 | 12 |
| 16 | 17 | 18 | 19 |
| 23 | 24 | 25 | 26 |

# June 2025

| FRIDAY | SATURDAY | SUNDAY | NOTES |
|---|---|---|---|
|  |  | 1 | ○ |
|  |  |  | ○ |
|  |  |  | ○ |
|  |  |  | ○ |
|  |  |  | ○ |
| 6 | 7 | 8 | ○ |
|  |  |  | ○ |
|  |  |  | ○ |
|  |  |  | ○ |
| 13 | 14 | 15 | ○ |
|  |  |  | ○ |
|  |  |  | ○ |
|  |  |  | ○ |
|  |  |  | ○ |
| 20 | 21 | 22 | ○ |
|  |  |  | ○ |
|  |  |  | ○ |
|  |  |  | ○ |
|  |  |  | ○ |
| 27 | 28 | 29 | 30 |

# July 2025

| MONDAY | TUESDAY | WEDNESDAY | THURSDAY |
|---|---|---|---|
|  | 1 | 2 | 3 |
| 7 | 8 | 9 | 10 |
| 14 | 15 | 16 | 17 |
| 21 | 22 | 23 | 24 |
| 28 | 29 | 30 | 31 |

# July 2025

| FRIDAY | SATURDAY | SUNDAY | NOTES |
|---|---|---|---|
| 4 | 5 | 6 | ○ |
| 11 | 12 | 13 | ○ |
| 18 | 19 | 20 | ○ |
| 25 | 26 | 27 | ○ |
|  |  |  | NOTES |

# August 2025

| MONDAY | TUESDAY | WEDNESDAY | THURSDAY |
|---|---|---|---|
|  |  |  |  |
| 4 | 5 | 6 | 7 |
| 11 | 12 | 13 | 14 |
| 18 | 19 | 20 | 21 |
| 25 | 26 | 27 | 28 |

# August 2025

| FRIDAY | SATURDAY | SUNDAY | NOTES |
|---|---|---|---|
| 1 | 2 | 3 | ○ |
| | | | ○ |
| | | | ○ |
| | | | ○ |
| | | | ○ |
| 8 | 9 | 10 | ○ |
| | | | ○ |
| | | | ○ |
| | | | ○ |
| | | | ○ |
| 15 | 16 | 17 | ○ |
| | | | ○ |
| | | | ○ |
| | | | ○ |
| | | | ○ |
| 22 | 23 | 24 | NOTES |
| 29 | 30 | 31 | |

# September 2025

| MONDAY | TUESDAY | WEDNESDAY | THURSDAY |
| --- | --- | --- | --- |
| 1 | 2 | 3 | 4 |
| 8 | 9 | 10 | 11 |
| 15 | 16 | 17 | 18 |
| 22 | 23 | 24 | 25 |
| 29 | 30 | | |

| FRIDAY | SATURDAY | SUNDAY | NOTES |
|---|---|---|---|
| 5 | 6 | 7 | ○ |
|  |  |  | ○ |
|  |  |  | ○ |
|  |  |  | ○ |
|  |  |  | ○ |
| 12 | 13 | 14 | ○ |
|  |  |  | ○ |
|  |  |  | ○ |
|  |  |  | ○ |
| 19 | 20 | 21 | ○ |
|  |  |  | ○ |
|  |  |  | ○ |
|  |  |  | ○ |
|  |  |  | ○ |
| 26 | 27 | 28 | ○ |
|  |  |  | ○ |
|  |  |  | ○ |
|  |  |  | ○ |
|  |  |  | ○ |
|  |  |  | NOTES |

# October 2025

| MONDAY | TUESDAY | WEDNESDAY | THURSDAY |
|---|---|---|---|
|  |  | 1 | 2 |
| 6 | 7 | 8 | 9 |
| 13 | 14 | 15 | 16 |
| 20 | 21 | 22 | 23 |
| 27 | 28 | 29 | 30 |

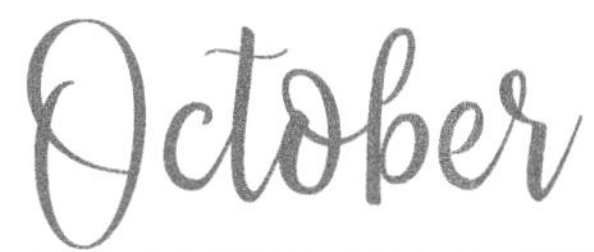

# October 2025

| FRIDAY | SATURDAY | SUNDAY | NOTES |
| --- | --- | --- | --- |
| 3 | 4 | 5 | ○ |
| | | | ○ |
| | | | ○ |
| | | | ○ |
| | | | ○ |
| 10 | 11 | 12 | ○ |
| | | | ○ |
| | | | ○ |
| | | | ○ |
| | | | ○ |
| 17 | 18 | 19 | ○ |
| | | | ○ |
| | | | ○ |
| | | | ○ |
| | | | ○ |
| 24 | 25 | 26 | ○ |
| | | | ○ |
| | | | ○ |
| | | | ○ |
| | | | ○ |
| 31 | | | NOTES |

# November 2025

| MONDAY | TUESDAY | WEDNESDAY | THURSDAY |
|---|---|---|---|
|  |  |  |  |
| 3 | 4 | 5 | 6 |
| 10 | 11 | 12 | 13 |
| 17 | 18 | 19 | 20 |
| 24 | 25 | 26 | 27 |

# November 2025

| FRIDAY | SATURDAY | SUNDAY | NOTES |
|---|---|---|---|
|  | 1 | 2 | ○ |
| 7 | 8 | 9 | ○ |
| 14 | 15 | 16 | ○ |
| 21 | 22 | 23 | ○ |
| 28 | 29 | 30 | NOTES |

# December *2025*

| THURSDAY | TUESDAY | WEDNESDAY | THURSDAY |
|---|---|---|---|
| 1 | 2 | 3 | 4 |
| 8 | 9 | 10 | 11 |
| 15 | 16 | 17 | 18 |
| 22 | 23 | 24 | 25 |
| 29 | 30 | 31 | |

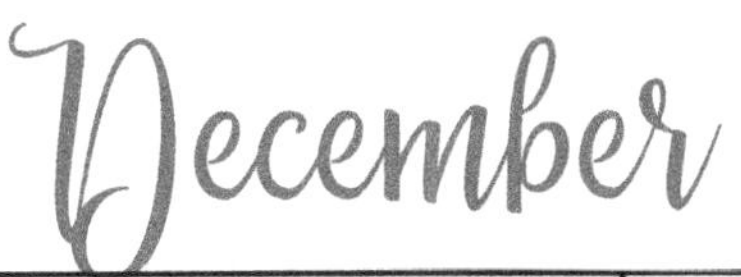

# December 2025

| FRIDAY | SATURDAY | SUNDAY | NOTES |
|---|---|---|---|
| 5 | 6 | 7 | ○ |
|  |  |  | ○ |
|  |  |  | ○ |
|  |  |  | ○ |
|  |  |  | ○ |
| 12 | 13 | 14 | ○ |
|  |  |  | ○ |
|  |  |  | ○ |
|  |  |  | ○ |
| 19 | 20 | 21 | ○ |
|  |  |  | ○ |
|  |  |  | ○ |
|  |  |  | ○ |
|  |  |  | ○ |
| 26 | 27 | 28 | ○ |
|  |  |  | ○ |
|  |  |  | ○ |
|  |  |  | ○ |
|  |  |  | ○ |
|  |  |  | NOTES |

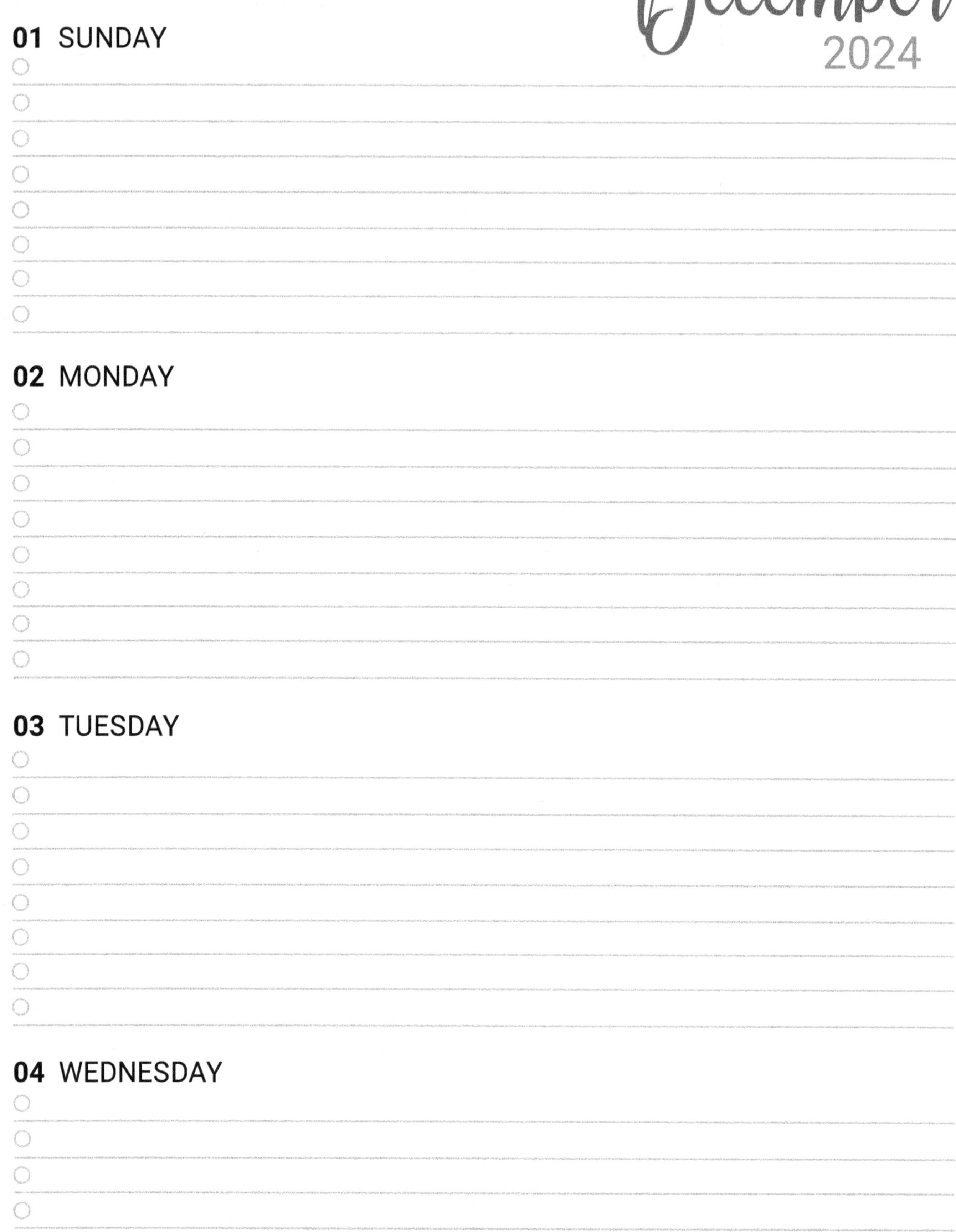



**01** SUNDAY

**02** MONDAY

**03** TUESDAY

**04** WEDNESDAY

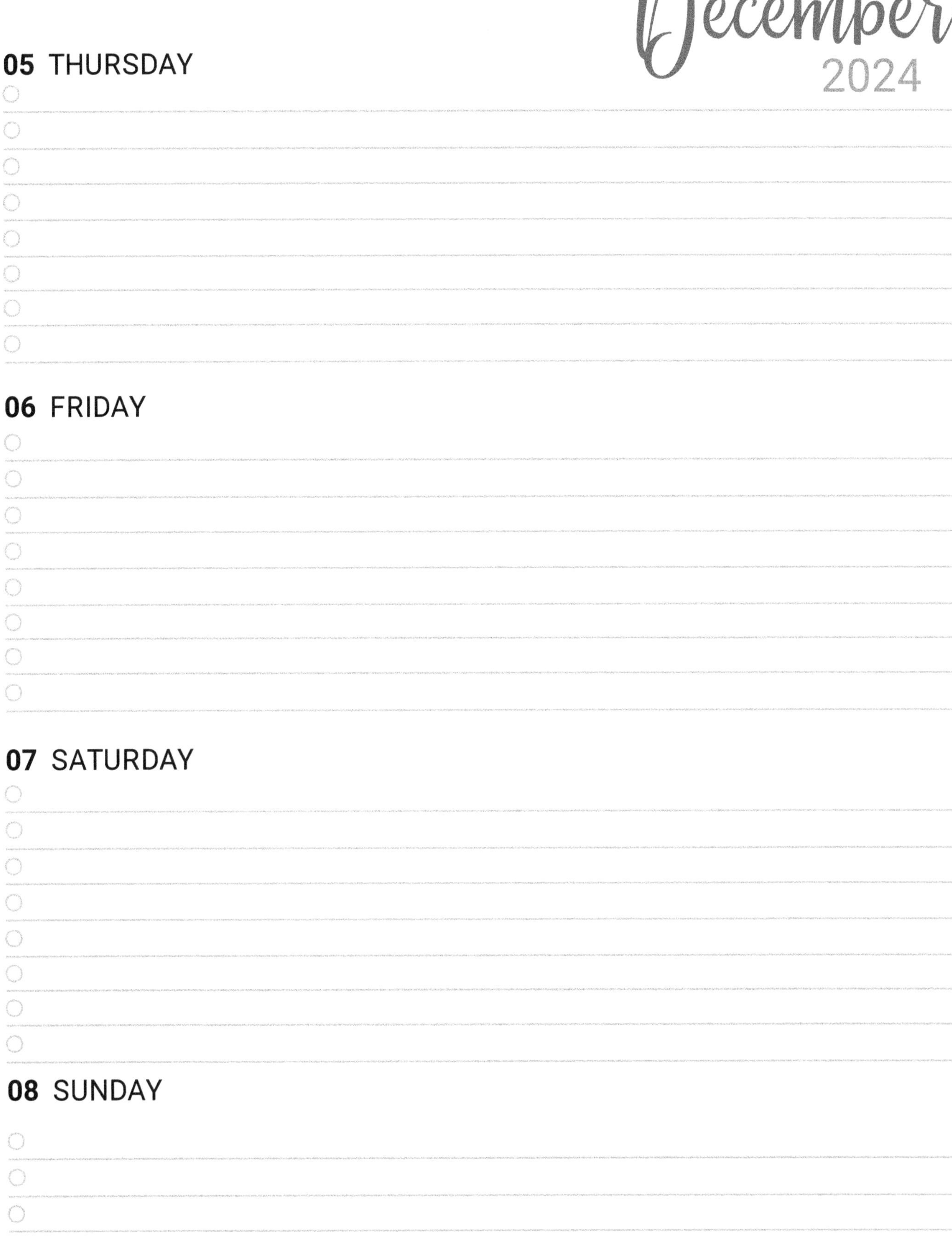



**05** THURSDAY

**06** FRIDAY

**07** SATURDAY

**08** SUNDAY

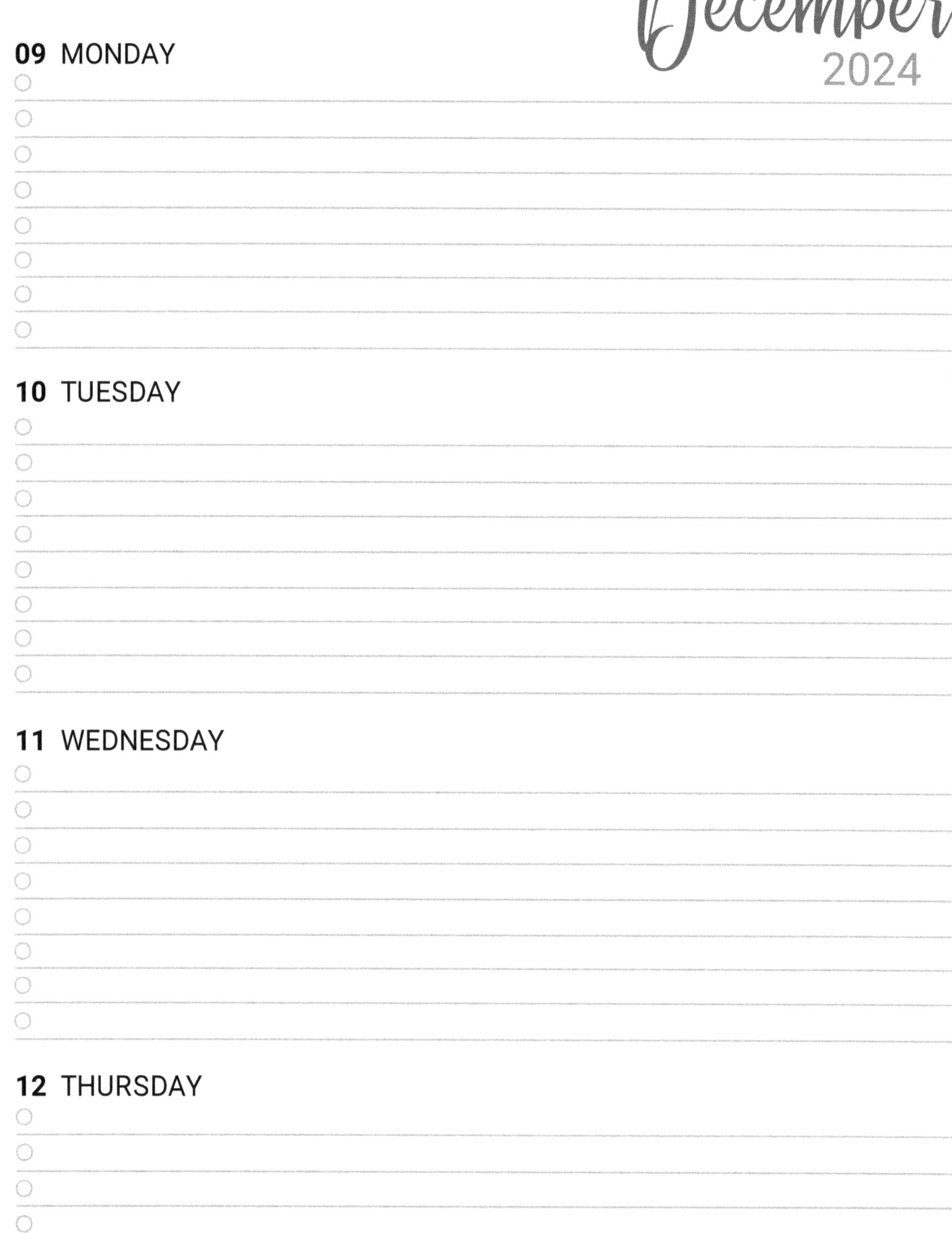

**09** MONDAY

**10** TUESDAY

**11** WEDNESDAY

**12** THURSDAY

December
2024

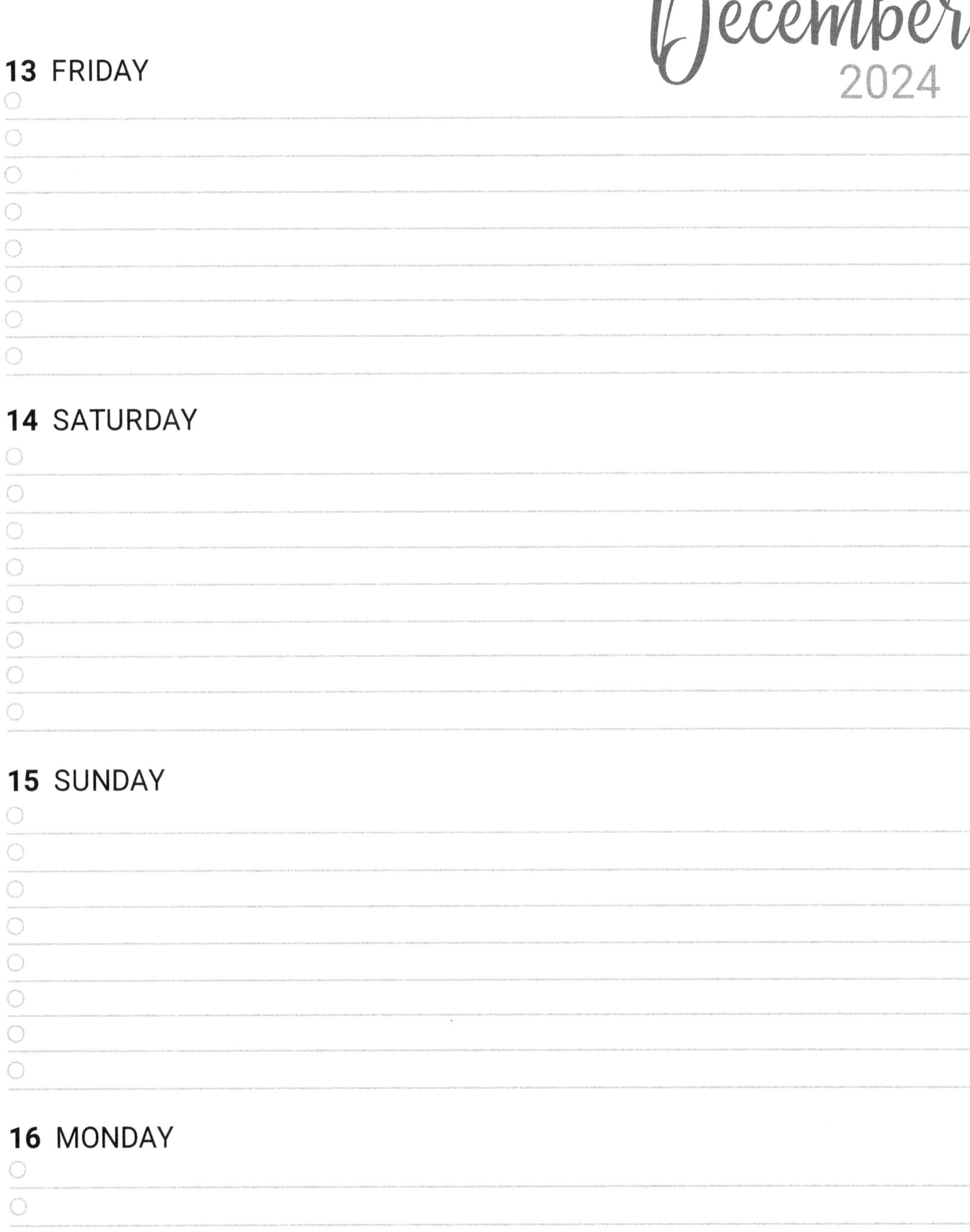



**13** FRIDAY

**14** SATURDAY

**15** SUNDAY

**16** MONDAY

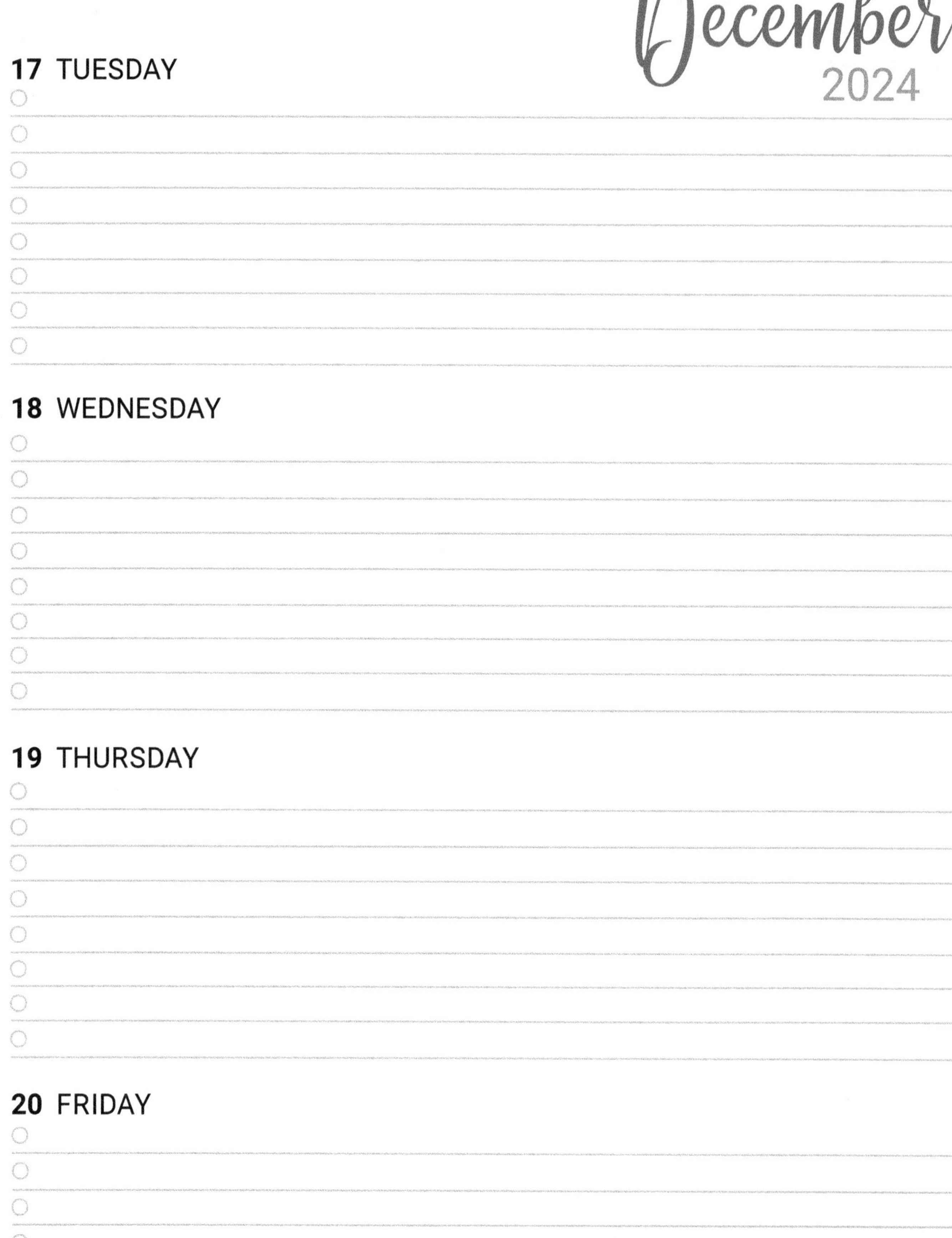

# December
## 2024

**17** TUESDAY

**18** WEDNESDAY

**19** THURSDAY

**20** FRIDAY

**21** SATURDAY

**22** SUNDAY

**23** MONDAY

**24** TUESDAY

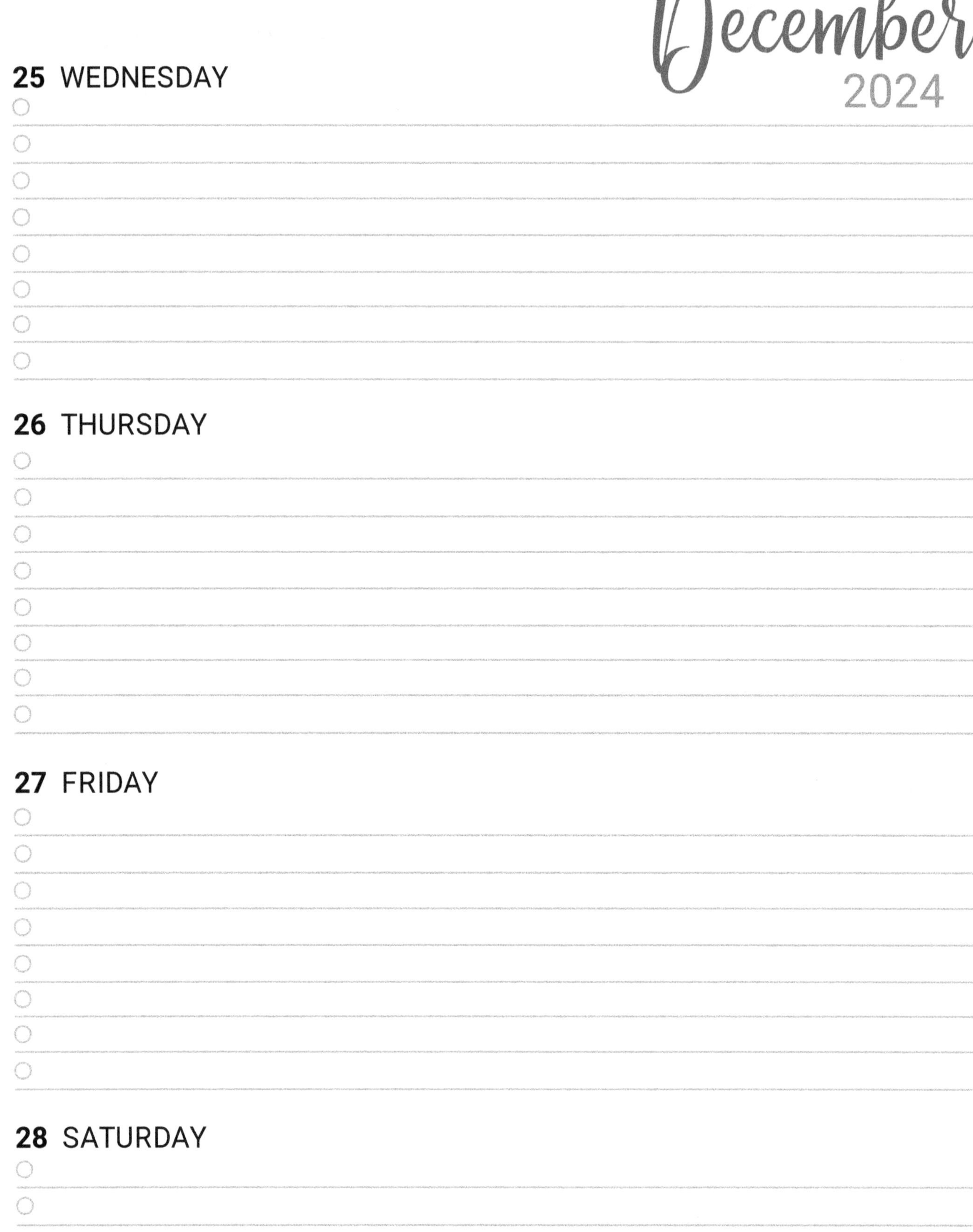

**25** WEDNESDAY

**26** THURSDAY

**27** FRIDAY

**28** SATURDAY

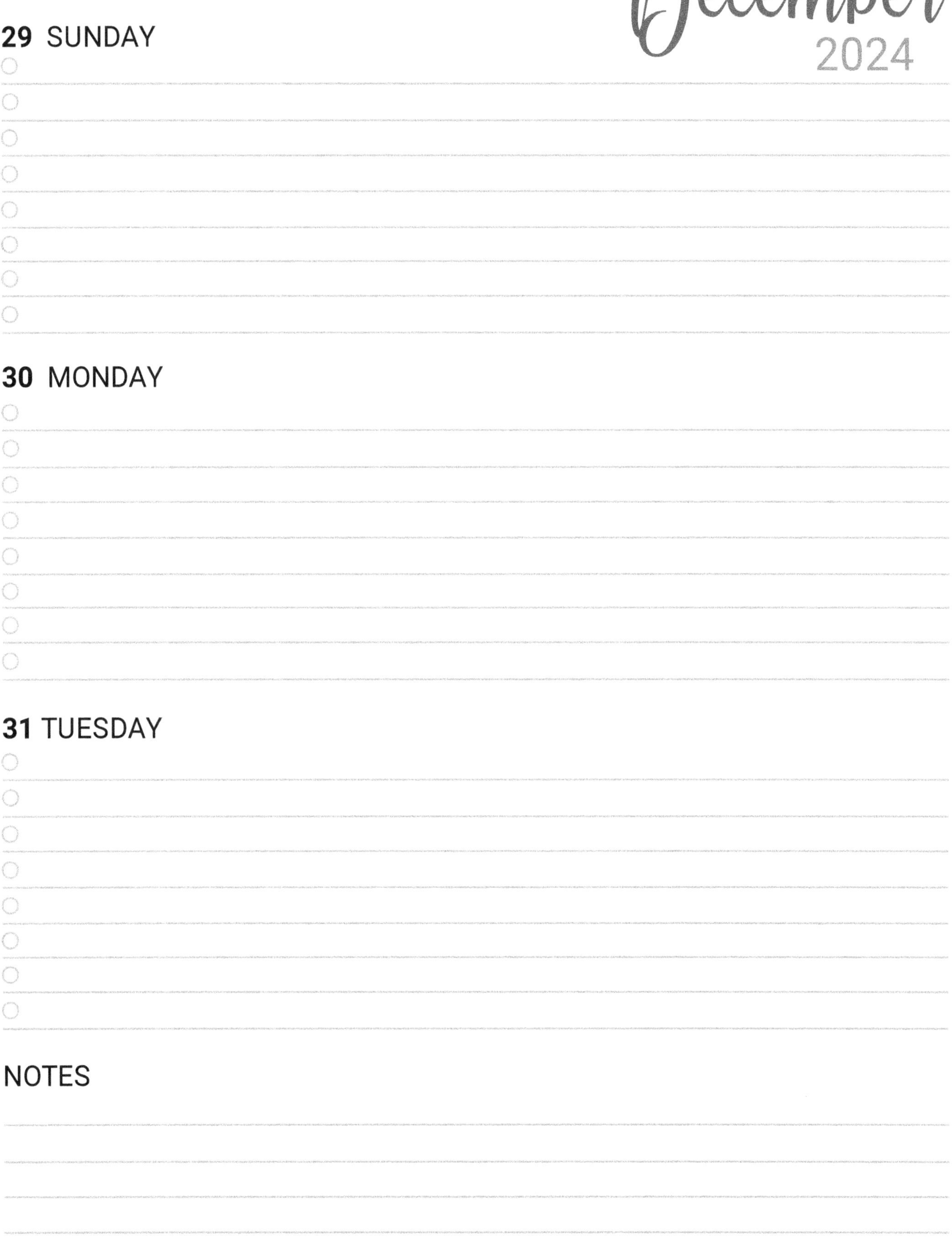

# December
## 2024

**29** SUNDAY

**30** MONDAY

**31** TUESDAY

NOTES

## 01 WEDNESDAY

## 02 THURSDAY

## 03 FRIDAY

## 04 SATURDAY

## 05 SUNDAY

## 06 MONDAY

## 07 TUESDAY

## 08 WEDNESDAY

**09** THURSDAY

**10** FRIDAY

**11** SATURDAY

**12** SUNDAY

**13** MONDAY

**14** TUESDAY

**15** WEDNESDAY

**16** THURSDAY

**17** FRIDAY

**18** SATURDAY

**19** SUNDAY

**20** MONDAY

**21** TUESDAY

**22** WEDNESDAY

**23** THURSDAY

**24** FRIDAY

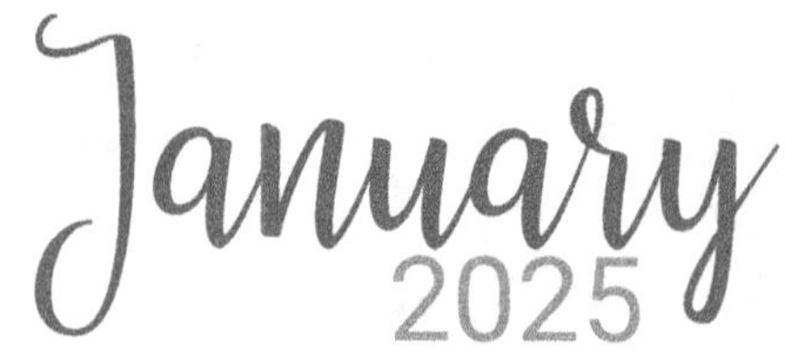

# January
## 2025

**25** SATURDAY

**26** SUNDAY

**27** MONDAY

**28** TUESDAY

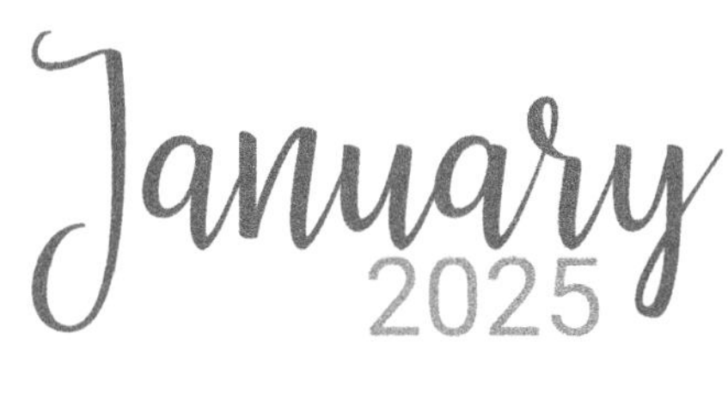



## 29 WEDNESDAY

○
○
○
○
○
○
○
○

## 30 THURSDAY

○
○
○
○
○
○
○
○

## 31 FRIDAY

○
○
○
○
○
○
○

## NOTES

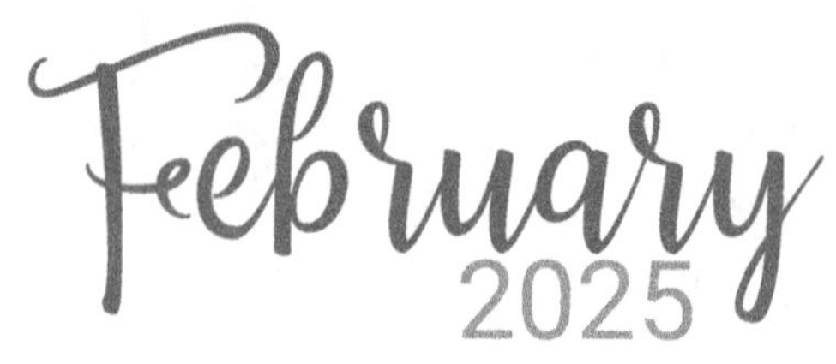


## 01 SATURDAY

## 02 SUNDAY

## 03 MONDAY

## 04 TUESDAY

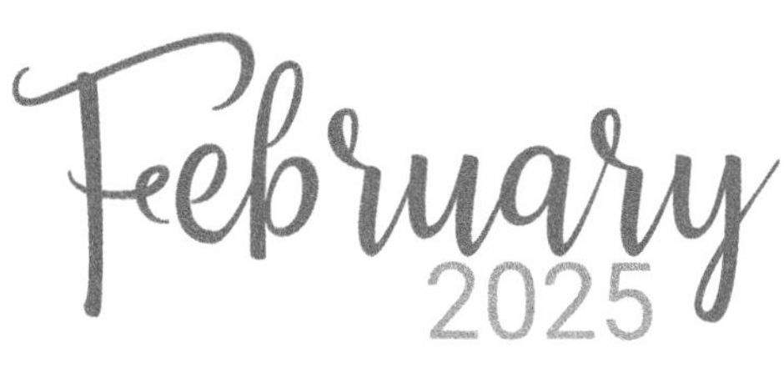


**05** WEDNESDAY

**06** THURSDAY

**07** FRIDAY

**08** SATURDAY

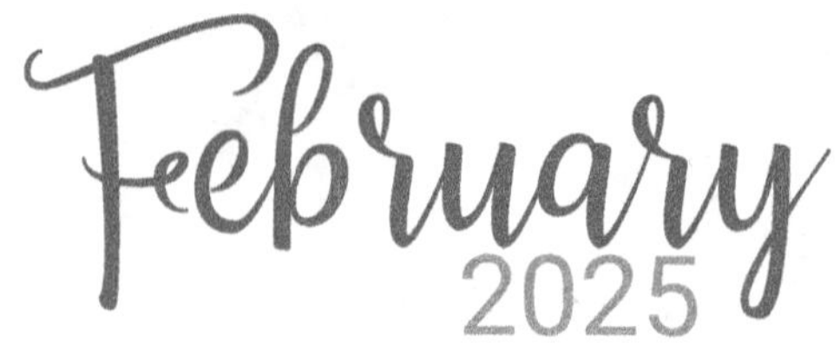


**09** SUNDAY

**10** MONDAY

**11** TUESDAY

**12** WEDNESDAY

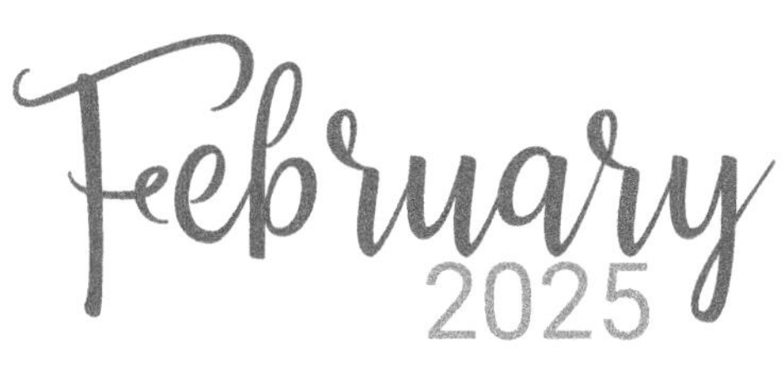


## 13 THURSDAY

## 14 FRIDAY

## 15 SATURDAY

## 16 SUNDAY

**17** MONDAY

**18** TUESDAY

**19** WEDNESDAY

**20** THURSDAY

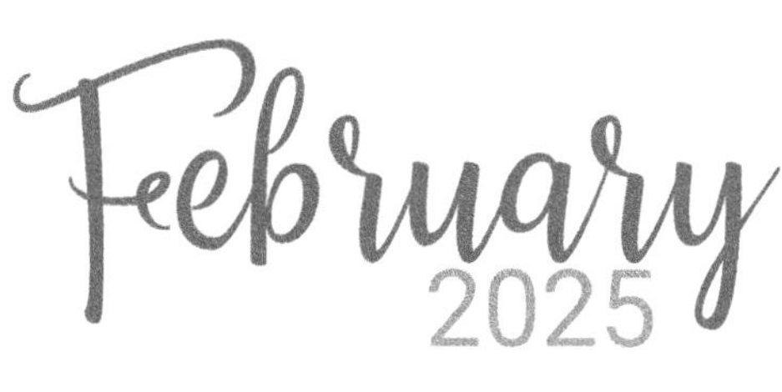


**21** FRIDAY

**22** SATURDAY

**23** SUNDAY

**24** MONDAY

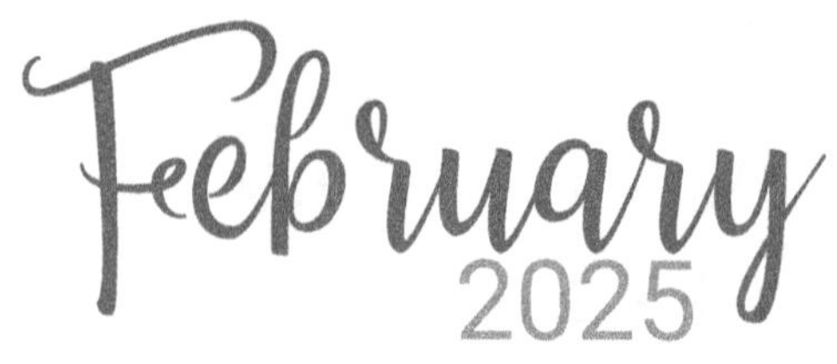

**February**
2025

**25** TUESDAY

**26** WEDNESDAY

**27** THURSDAY

**28** FRIDAY

## 01 SATURDAY

## 02 SUNDAY

## 03 MONDAY

## 04 TUESDAY

**05** WEDNESDAY

**06** THURSDAY

**07** FRIDAY

**08** SATURDAY

## 09 SUNDAY

## 10 MONDAY

## 11 TUESDAY

## 12 WEDNESDAY

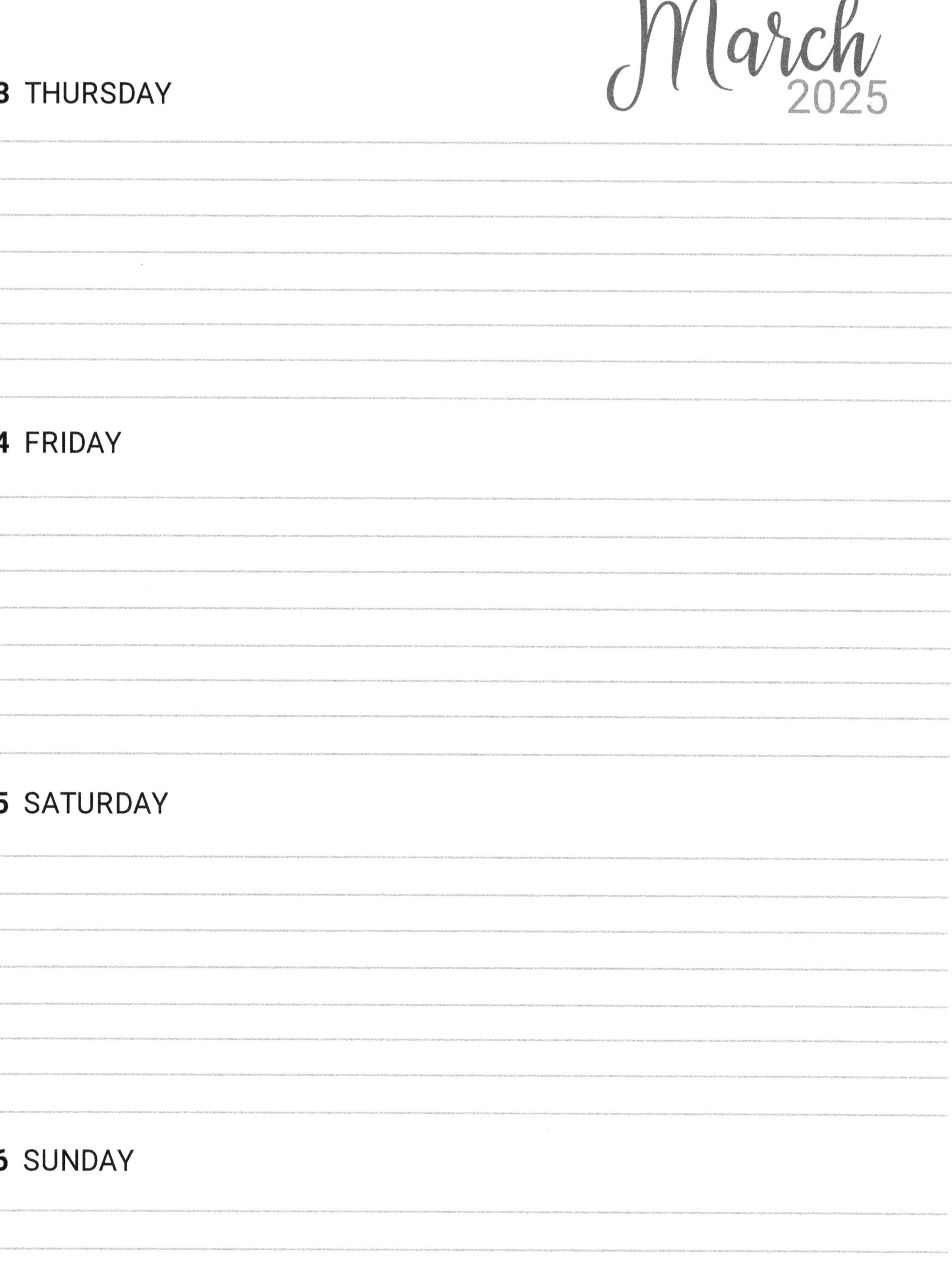



**13** THURSDAY

**14** FRIDAY

**15** SATURDAY

**16** SUNDAY

**17** MONDAY

**18** TUESDAY

**19** WEDNESDAY

**20** THURSDAY

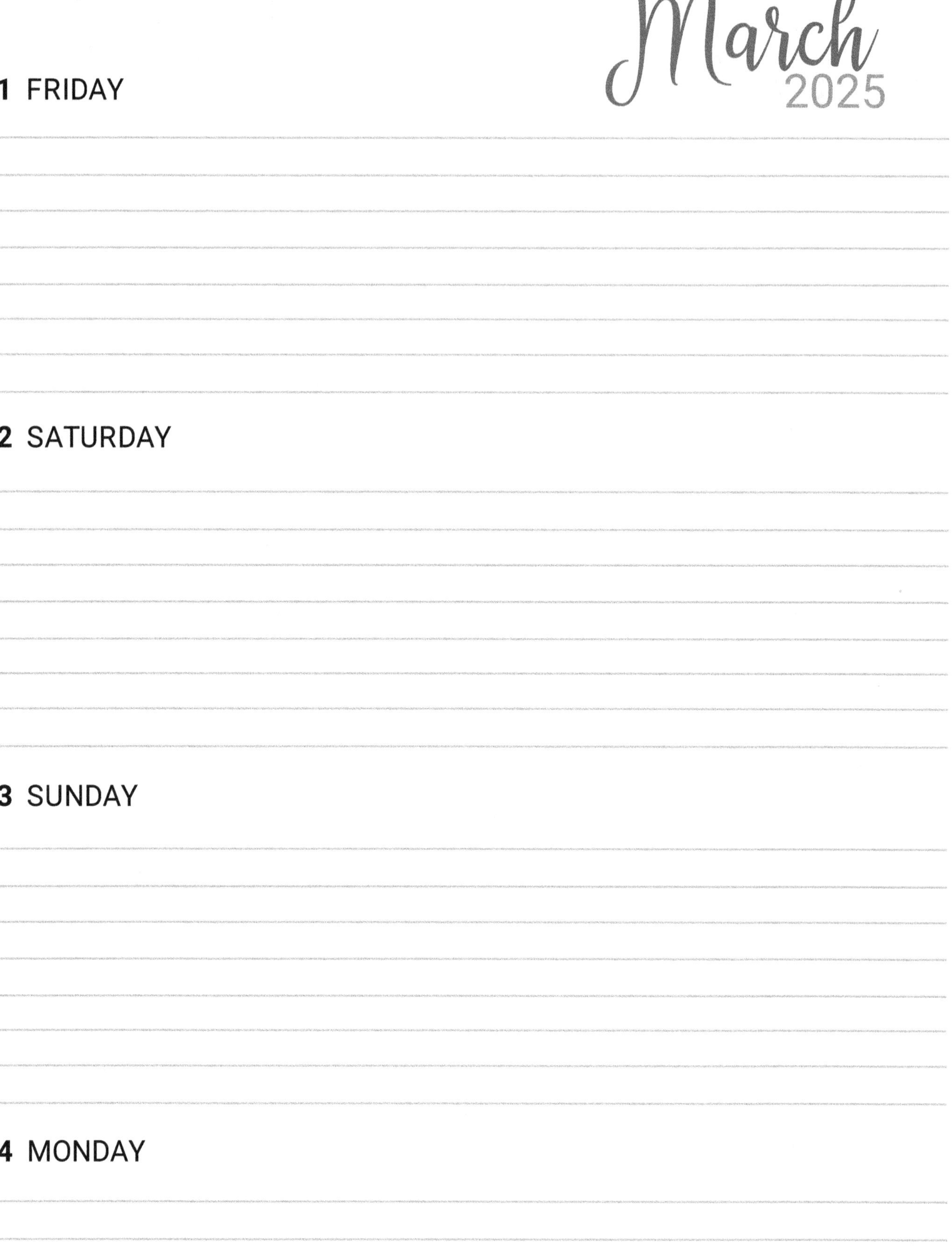



**21** FRIDAY

**22** SATURDAY

**23** SUNDAY

**24** MONDAY

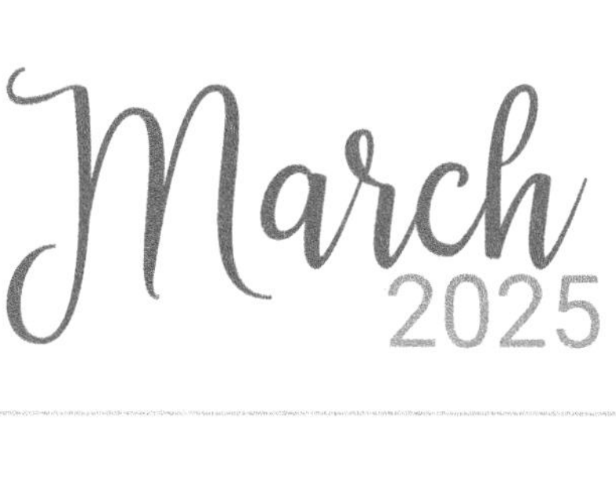


## 25 TUESDAY

## 26 WEDNESDAY

## 27 THURSDAY

## 28 FRIDAY

**29** SATURDAY

**30** SUNDAY

**31** MONDAY

NOTES

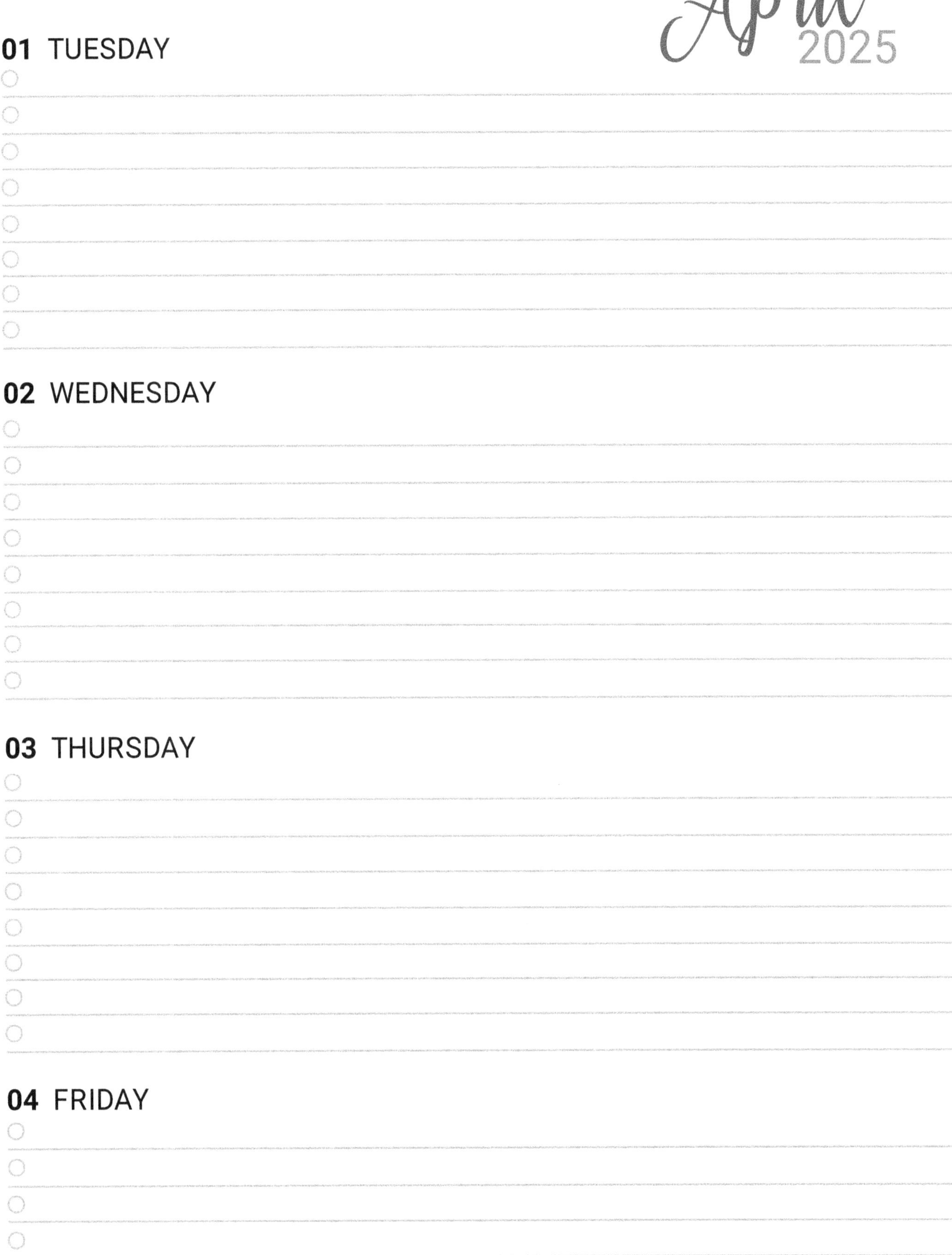



**01** TUESDAY

**02** WEDNESDAY

**03** THURSDAY

**04** FRIDAY

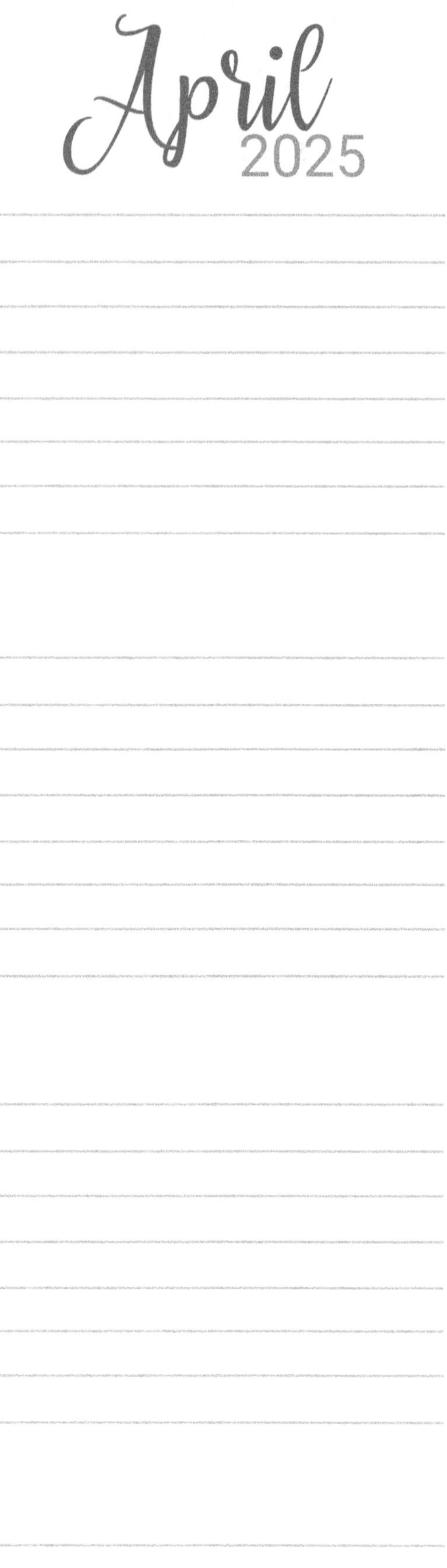


**05** SATURDAY

**06** SUNDAY

**07** MONDAY

**08** TUESDAY

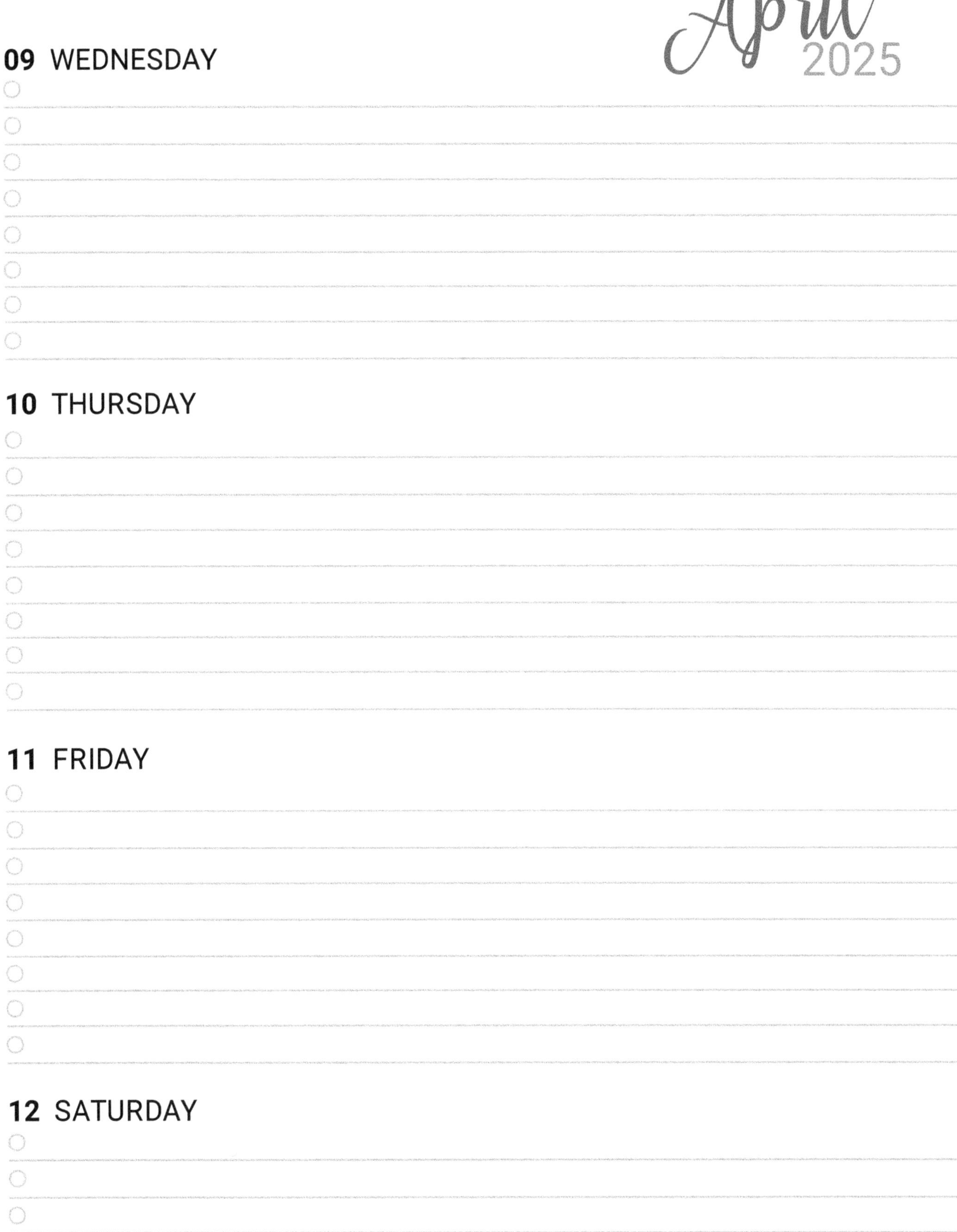



**09** WEDNESDAY

**10** THURSDAY

**11** FRIDAY

**12** SATURDAY

**13** SUNDAY

**14** MONDAY

**15** TUESDAY

**16** WEDNESDAY

## 17 THURSDAY

## 18 FRIDAY

## 19 SATURDAY

## 20 SUNDAY

## 21 MONDAY

## 22 TUESDAY

## 23 WEDNESDAY

## 24 THURSDAY

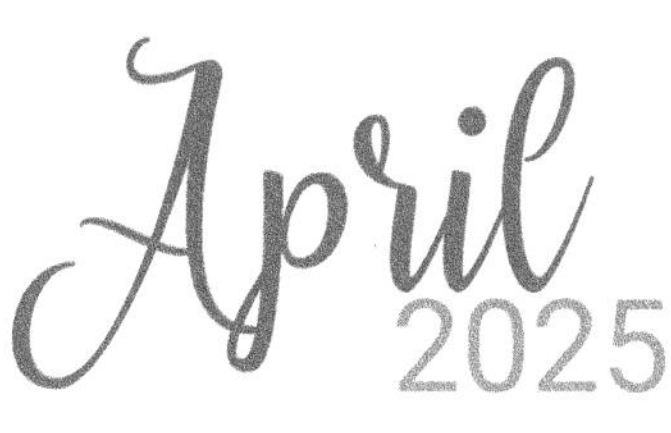

**25** FRIDAY

**26** SATURDAY

**27** SUNDAY

**28** MONDAY

**29** TUESDAY

**30** WEDNESDAY

NOTES

# May<br>2025

## 01 THURSDAY

## 02 FRIDAY

## 03 SATURDAY

## 04 SUNDAY

**05** MONDAY

**06** TUESDAY

**07** WEDNESDAY

**08** THURSDAY

**09** FRIDAY

**10** SATURDAY

**11** SUNDAY

**12** MONDAY

## 13 TUESDAY

## 14 WEDNESDAY

## 15 THURSDAY

## 16 FRIDAY

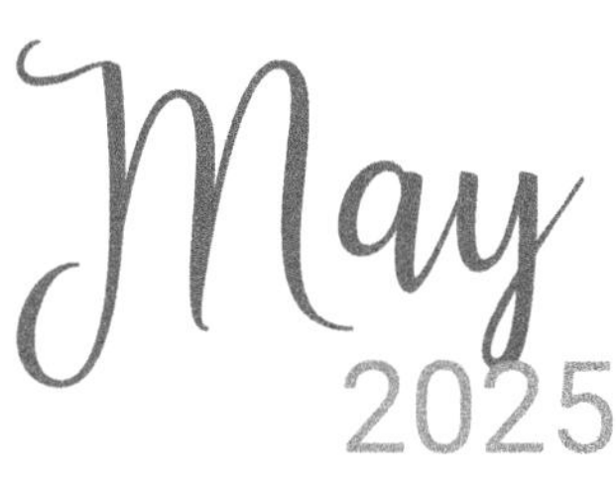


**17** SATURDAY

**18** SUNDAY

**19** MONDAY

**20** TUESDAY

**21** WEDNESDAY

**22** THURSDAY

**23** FRIDAY

**24** SATURDAY

# May
## 2025

**25** SUNDAY

**26** MONDAY

**27** TUESDAY

**28** WEDNESDAY

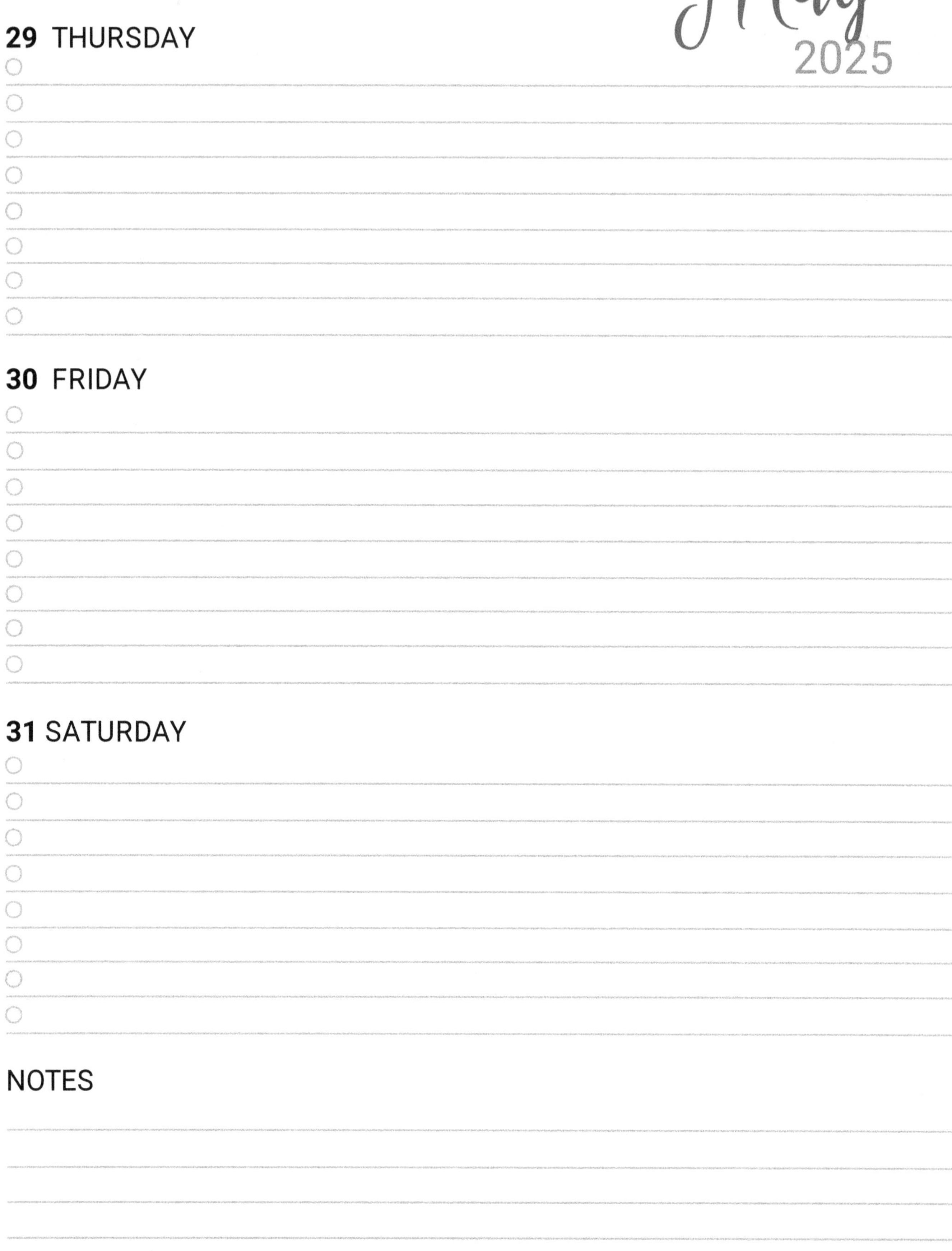

# May
## 2025

**29** THURSDAY

**30** FRIDAY

**31** SATURDAY

NOTES

# June

## 2025

**01** SUNDAY

**02** MONDAY

**03** TUESDAY

**04** WEDNESDAY

# June 2025

## 05 THURSDAY

## 06 FRIDAY

## 07 SATURDAY

## 08 SUNDAY

**09** MONDAY

**10** TUESDAY

**11** WEDNESDAY

**12** THURSDAY

# June
### 2025

**13** FRIDAY

○
○
○
○
○
○
○

**14** SATURDAY

○
○
○
○
○
○
○
○

**15** SUNDAY

○
○
○
○
○
○
○
○

**16** MONDAY

○
○
○
○
○

## 17 TUESDAY

## 18 WEDNESDAY

## 19 THURSDAY

## 20 FRIDAY

## 21 SATURDAY

## 22 SUNDAY

## 23 MONDAY

## 24 TUESDAY

## 25 WEDNESDAY

## 26 THURSDAY

## 27 FRIDAY

## 28 SATURDAY

# June 2025

## 29 SUNDAY

## 30 MONDAY

## NOTES

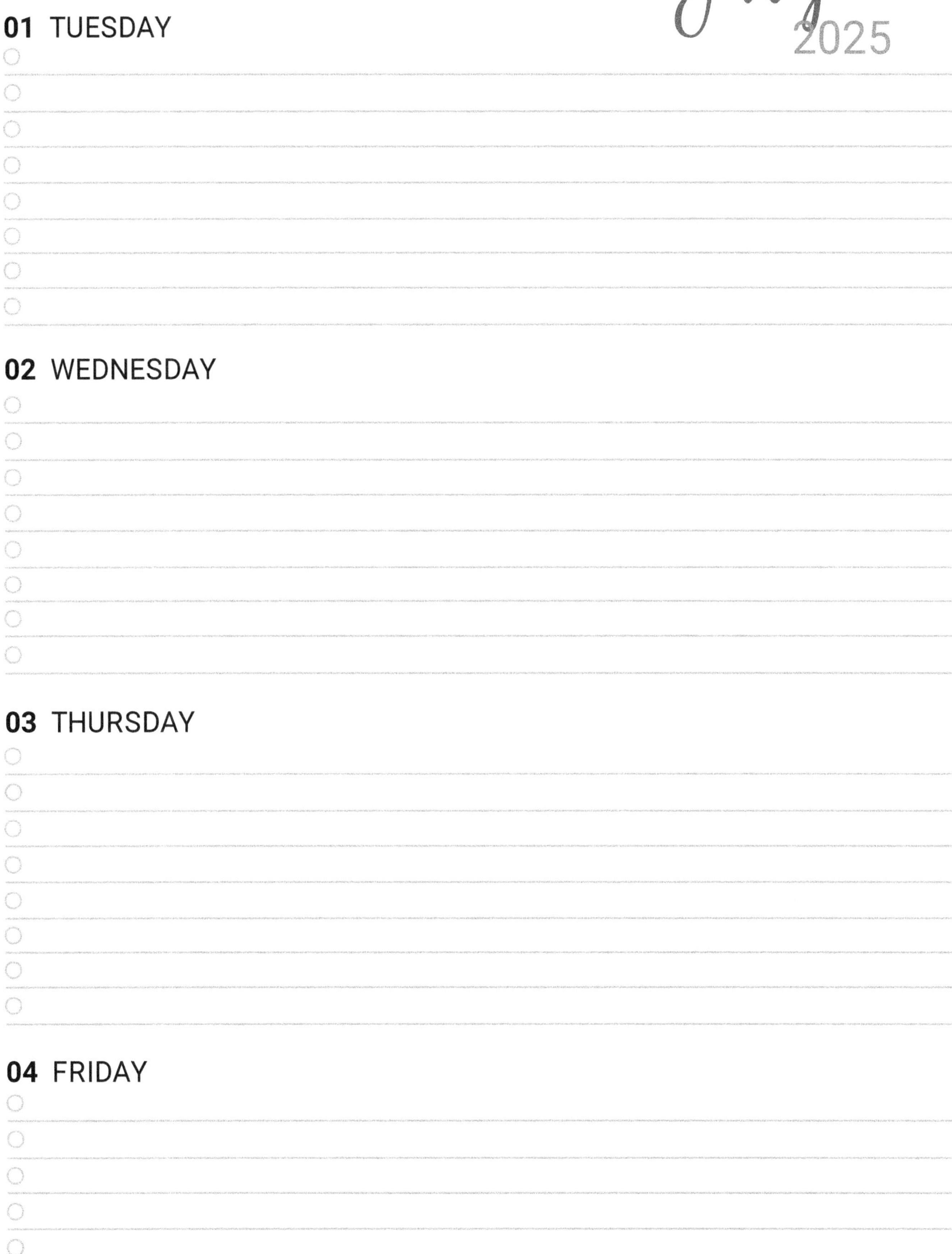

# July
## 2025

**01** TUESDAY

**02** WEDNESDAY

**03** THURSDAY

**04** FRIDAY

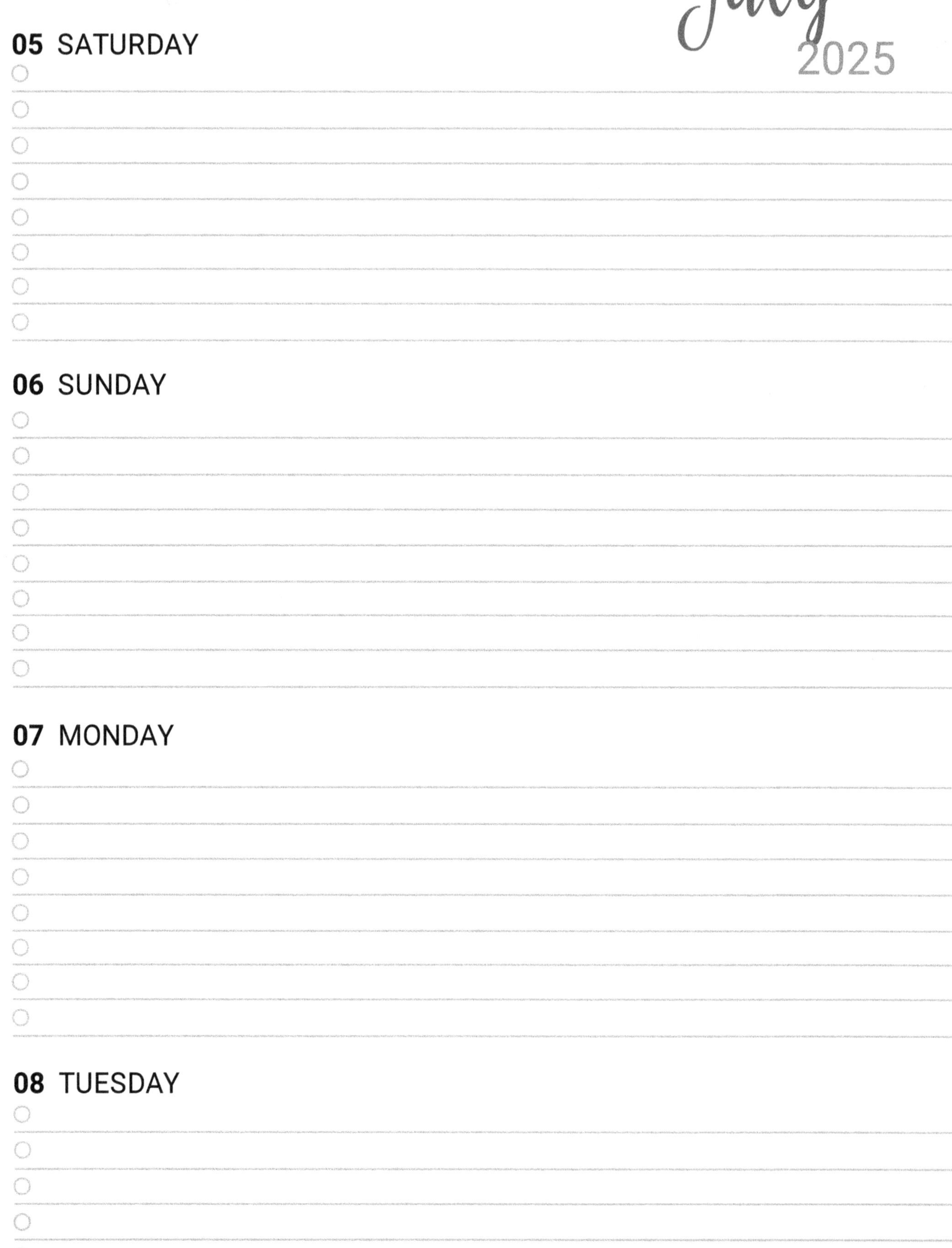



## 05 SATURDAY

## 06 SUNDAY

## 07 MONDAY

## 08 TUESDAY

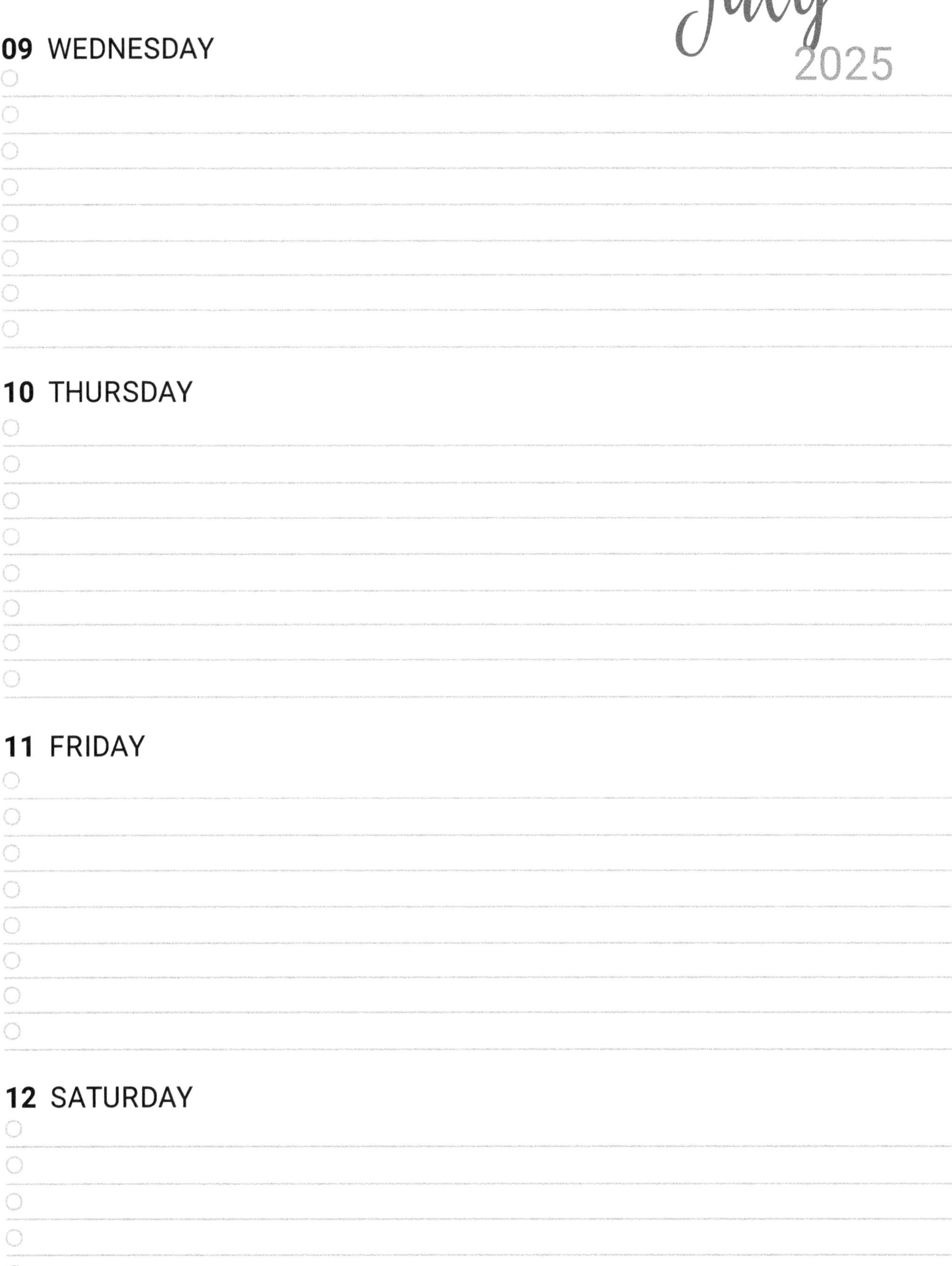



**09** WEDNESDAY

**10** THURSDAY

**11** FRIDAY

**12** SATURDAY

**13** SUNDAY

**14** MONDAY

**15** TUESDAY

**16** WEDNESDAY

## 17 THURSDAY

## 18 FRIDAY

## 19 SATURDAY

## 20 SUNDAY

**21** MONDAY

**22** TUESDAY

**23** WEDNESDAY

**24** THURSDAY

## 25 FRIDAY

## 26 SATURDAY

## 27 SUNDAY

## 28 MONDAY

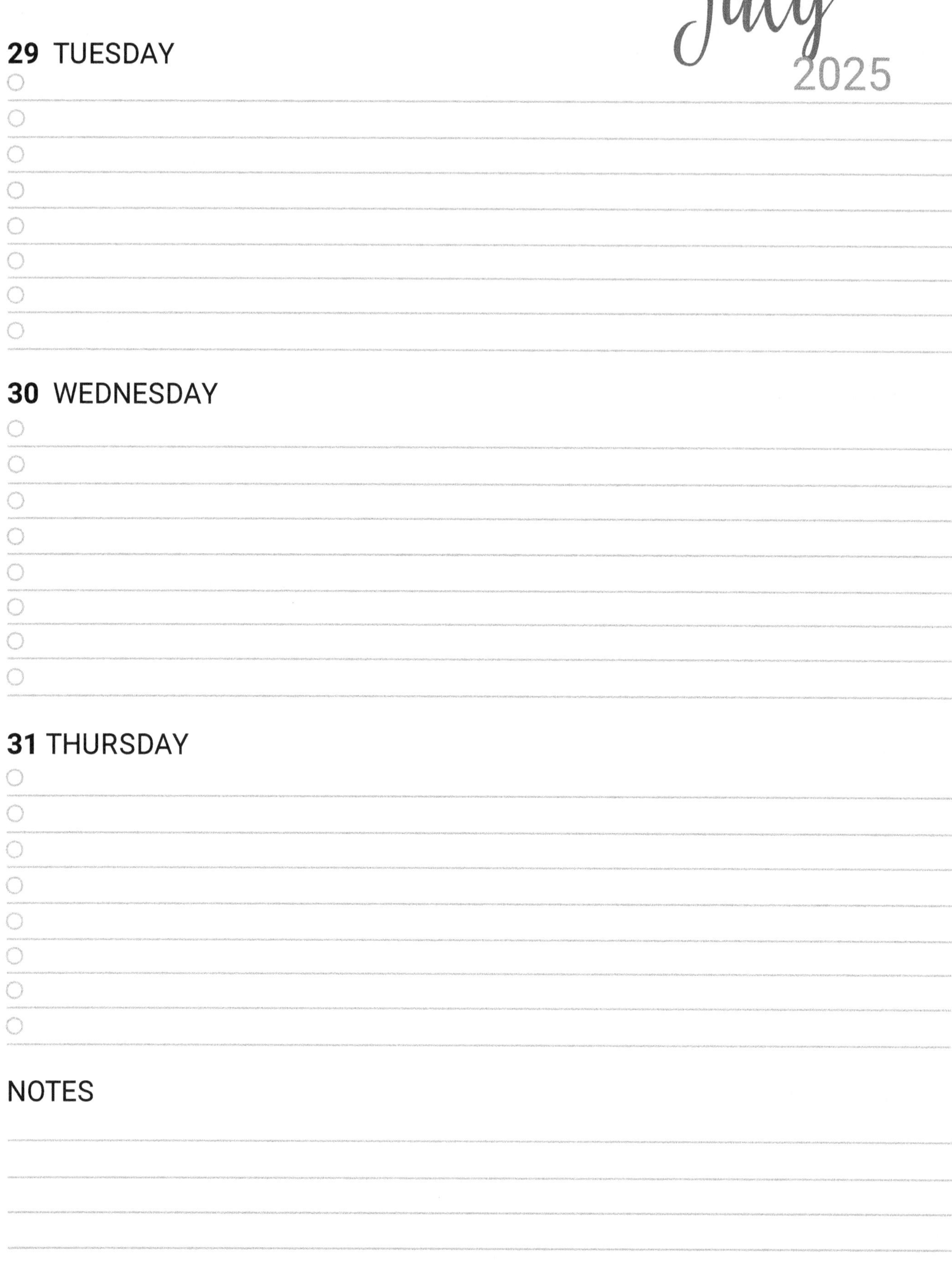

# July
## 2025

**29** TUESDAY

**30** WEDNESDAY

**31** THURSDAY

NOTES

**01** FRIDAY

**02** SATURDAY

**03** SUNDAY

**04** MONDAY

**05** TUESDAY

**06** WEDNESDAY

**07** THURSDAY

**08** FRIDAY

## 09 SATURDAY

## 10 SUNDAY

## 11 MONDAY

## 12 TUESDAY

**13** WEDNESDAY

**14** THURSDAY

**15** FRIDAY

**16** SATURDAY

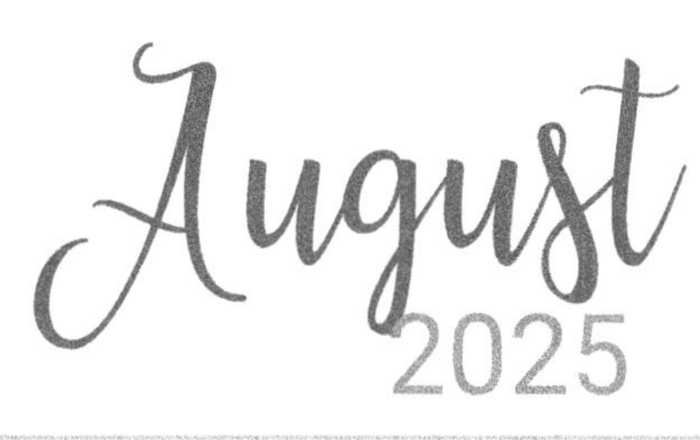


**17** SUNDAY

**18** MONDAY

**19** TUESDAY

**20** WEDNESDAY

## 21 THURSDAY

## 22 FRIDAY

## 23 SATURDAY

## 24 SUNDAY

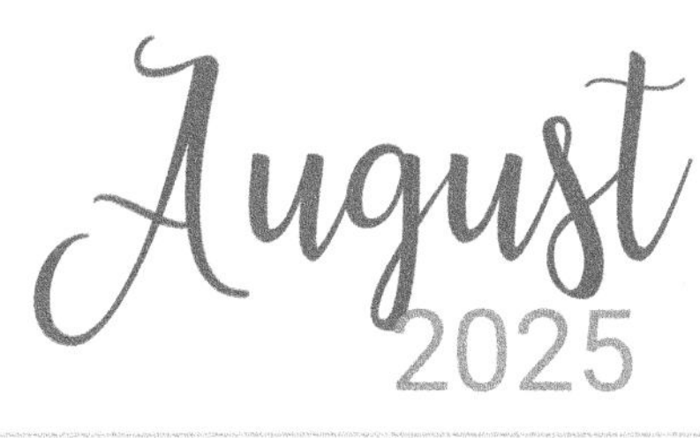


**25** MONDAY

**26** TUESDAY

**27** WEDNESDAY

**28** THURSDAY

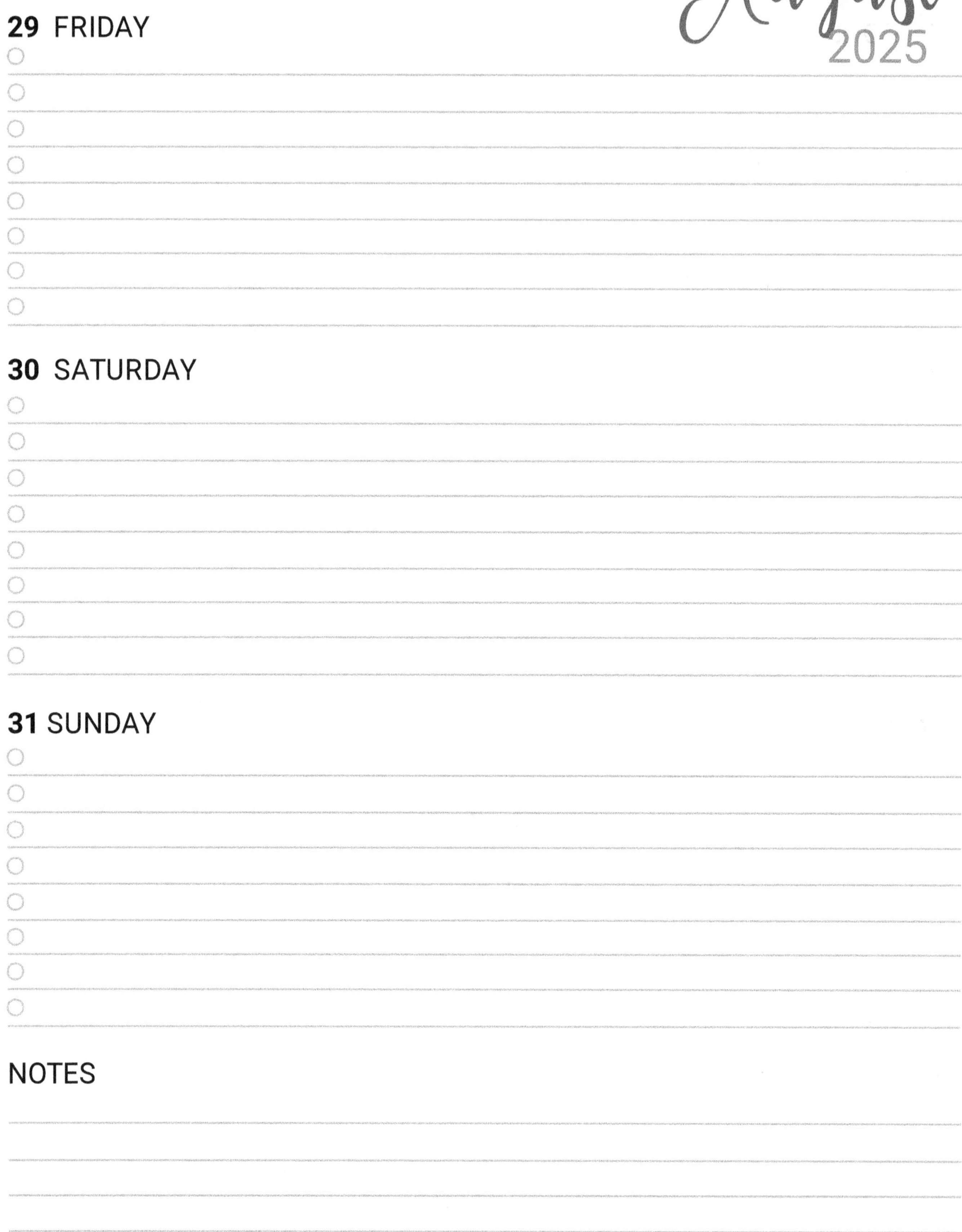


August
2025
29 FRIDAY
30 SATURDAY
31 SUNDAY
NOTES

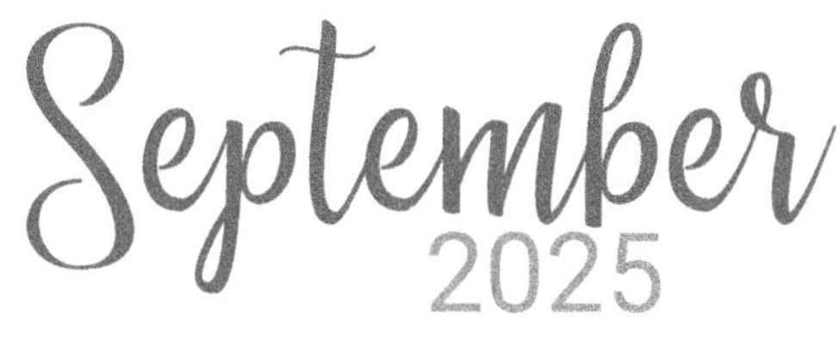


**01** MONDAY

**02** TUESDAY

**03** WEDNESDAY

**04** THURSDAY

**05** FRIDAY

**06** SATURDAY

**07** SUNDAY

**08** MONDAY

**09** TUESDAY

**10** WEDNESDAY

**11** THURSDAY

**12** FRIDAY

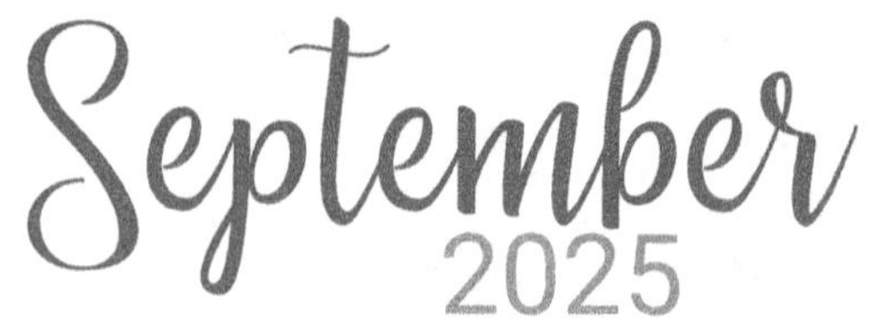


**13** SATURDAY

**14** SUNDAY

**15** MONDAY

**16** TUESDAY

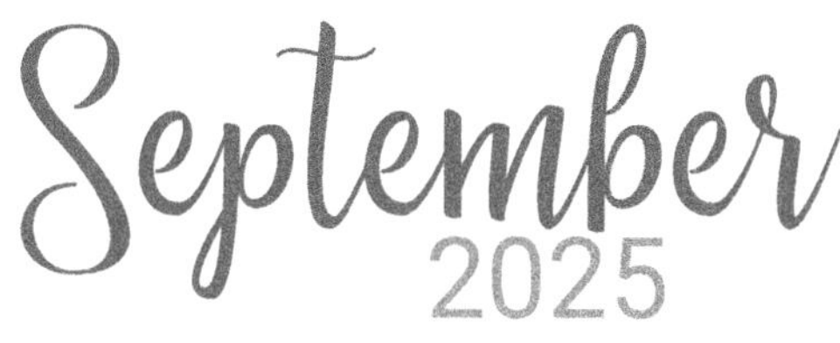

# September
## 2025

**17** WEDNESDAY

**18** THURSDAY

**19** FRIDAY

**20** SATURDAY

**21** SUNDAY

**22** MONDAY

**23** TUESDAY

**24** WEDNESDAY

**25** THURSDAY

**26** FRIDAY

**27** SATURDAY

**28** SUNDAY

**29** MONDAY

**30** TUESDAY

NOTES

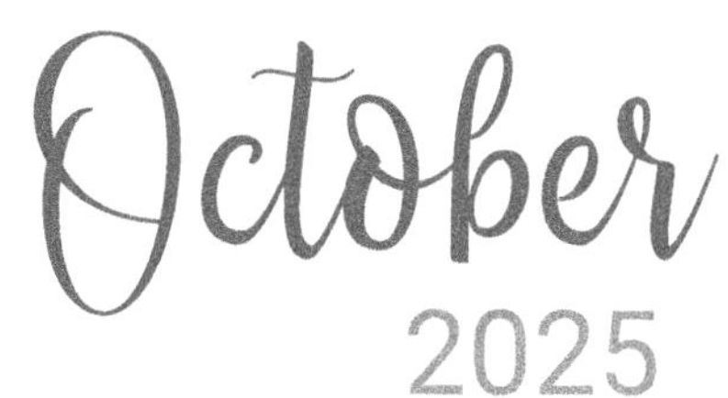

# October
## 2025

**01** WEDNESDAY

**02** THURSDAY

**03** FRIDAY

**04** SATURDAY

October
2025
05 SUNDAY
06 MONDAY
07 TUESDAY
08 WEDNESDAY

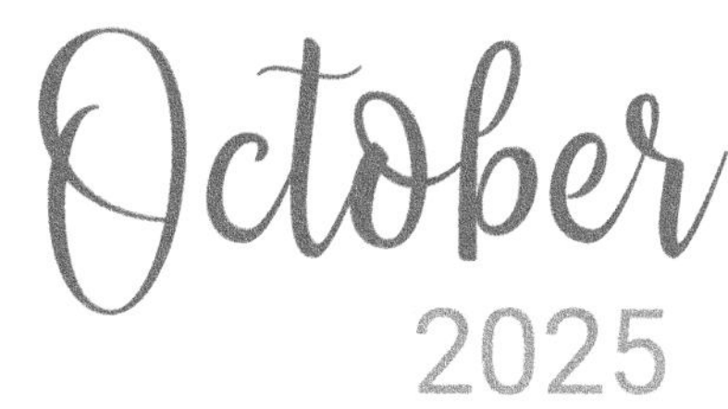



**09** THURSDAY

**10** FRIDAY

**11** SATURDAY

**12** SUNDAY

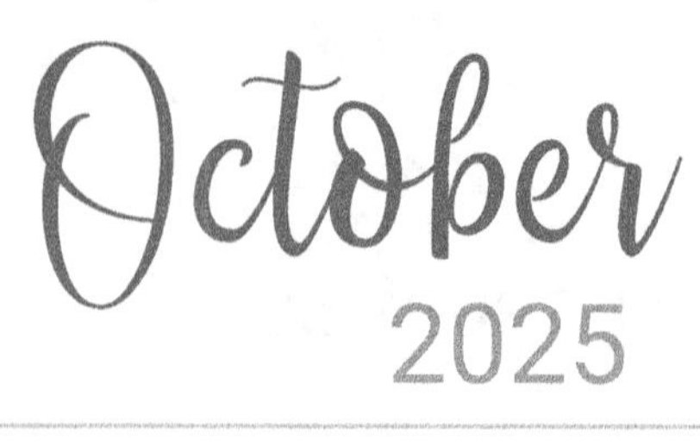

# October
## 2025

**13** MONDAY

**14** TUESDAY

**15** WEDNESDAY

**16** THURSDAY

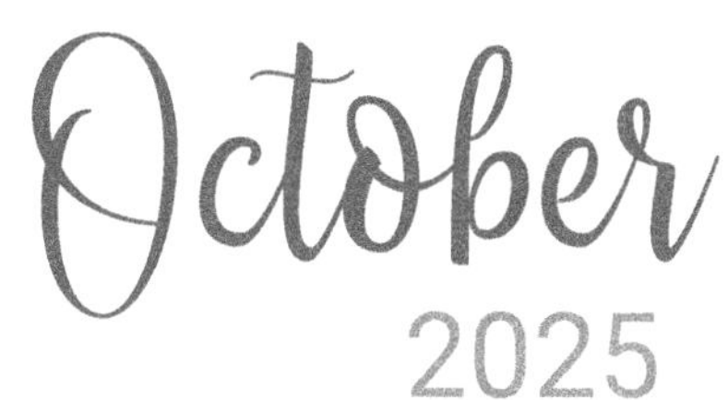


**17** FRIDAY

**18** SATURDAY

**19** SUNDAY

**20** MONDAY

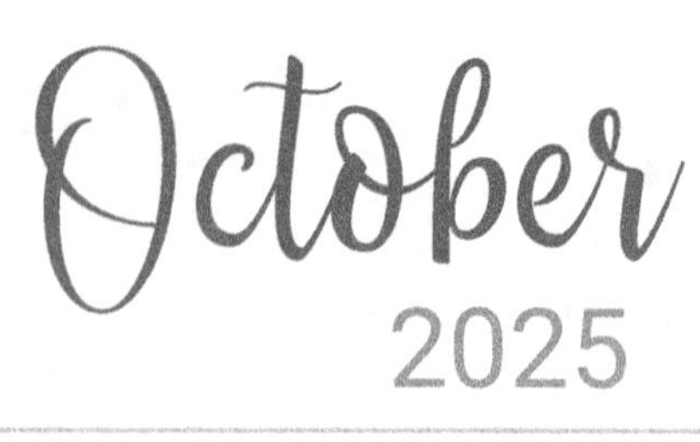


## 21 TUESDAY

## 22 WEDNESDAY

## 23 THURSDAY

## 24 FRIDAY

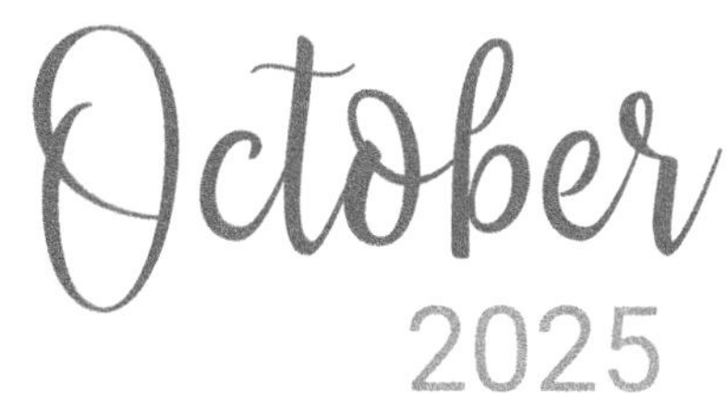



**25** SATURDAY

**26** SUNDAY

**27** MONDAY

**28** TUESDAY

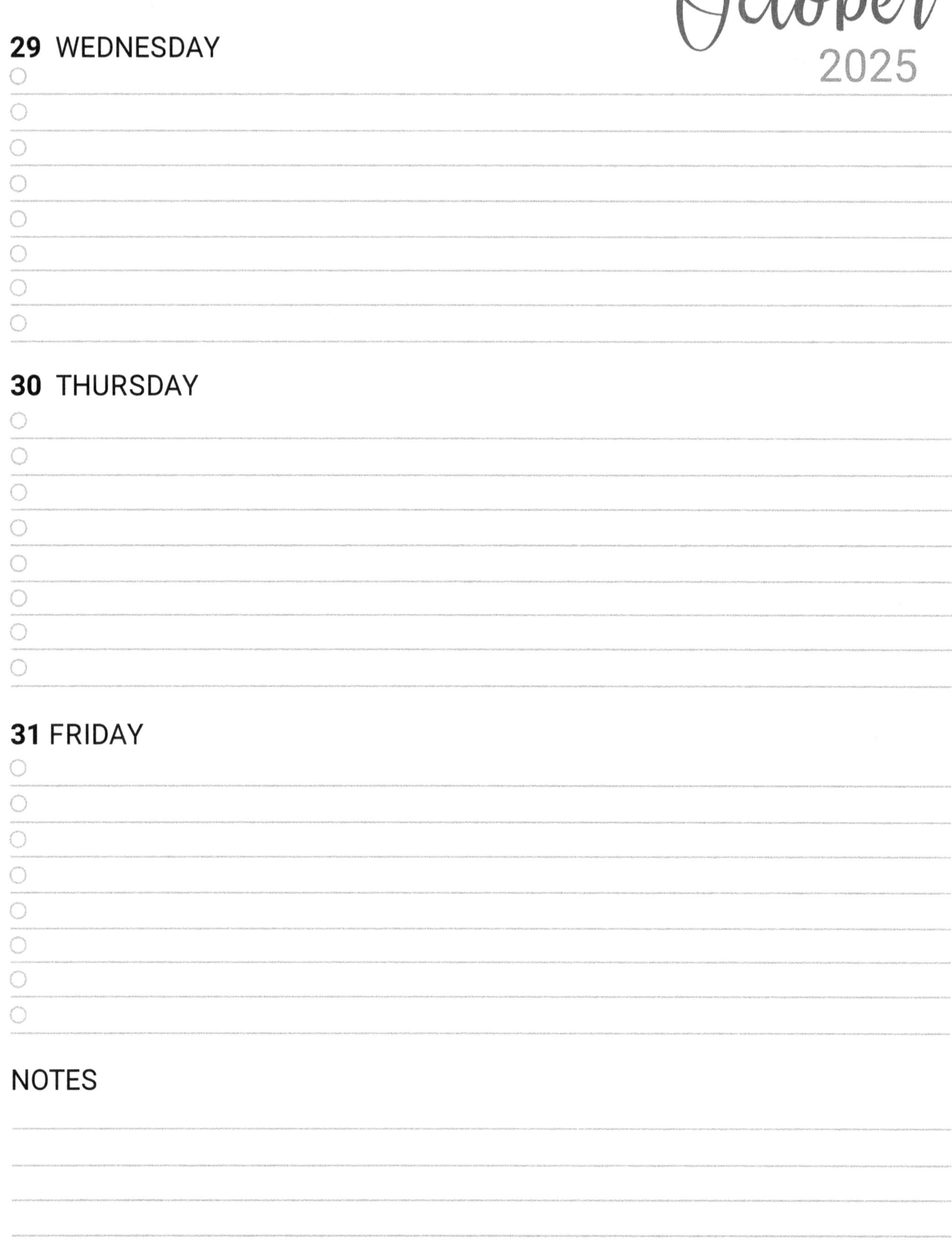

# October
### 2025

**29** WEDNESDAY

**30** THURSDAY

**31** FRIDAY

NOTES

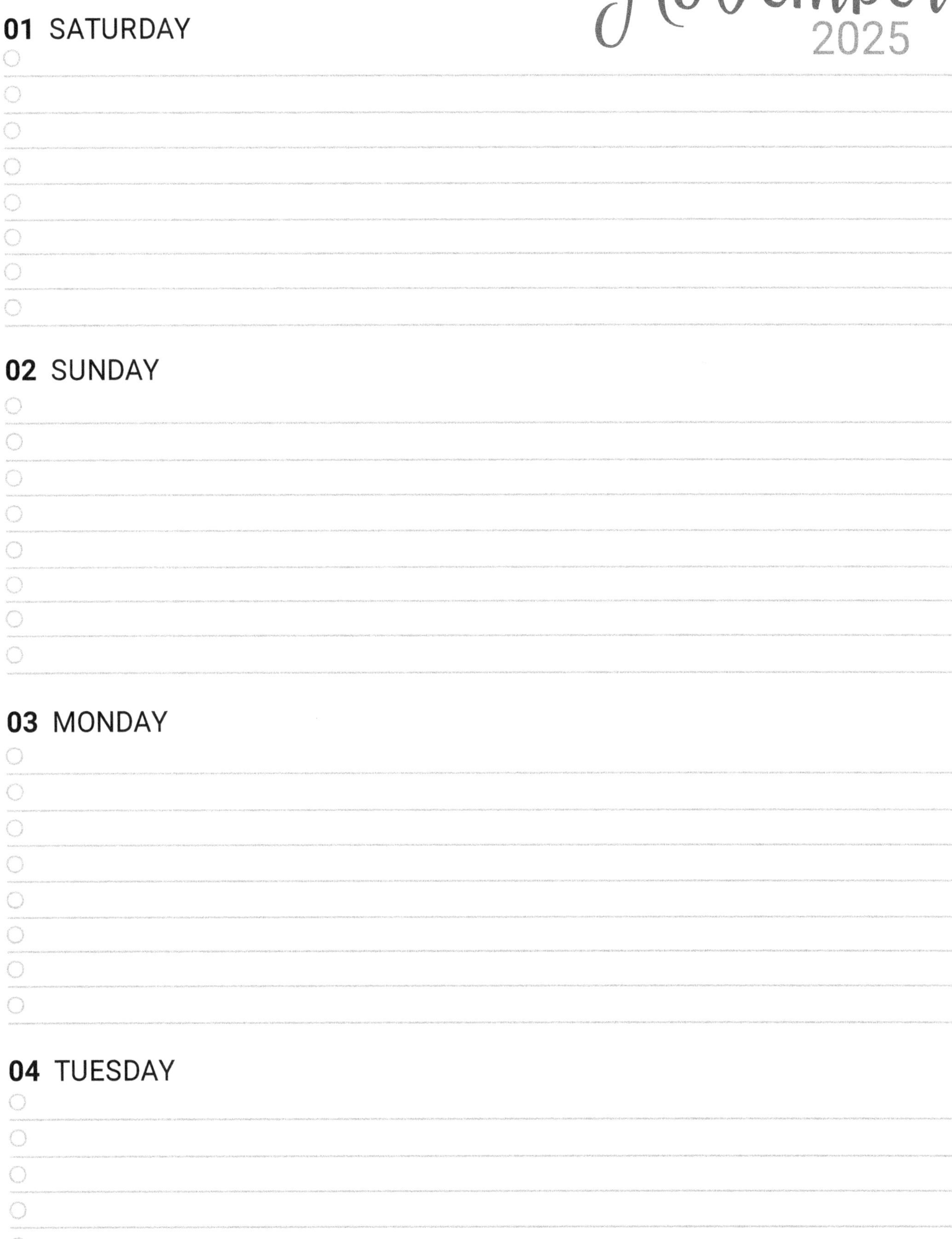



**01** SATURDAY

**02** SUNDAY

**03** MONDAY

**04** TUESDAY

**05** WEDNESDAY

**06** THURSDAY

**07** FRIDAY

**08** SATURDAY

**09** SUNDAY

**10** MONDAY

**11** TUESDAY

**12** WEDNESDAY

**13** THURSDAY

**14** FRIDAY

**15** SATURDAY

**16** SUNDAY

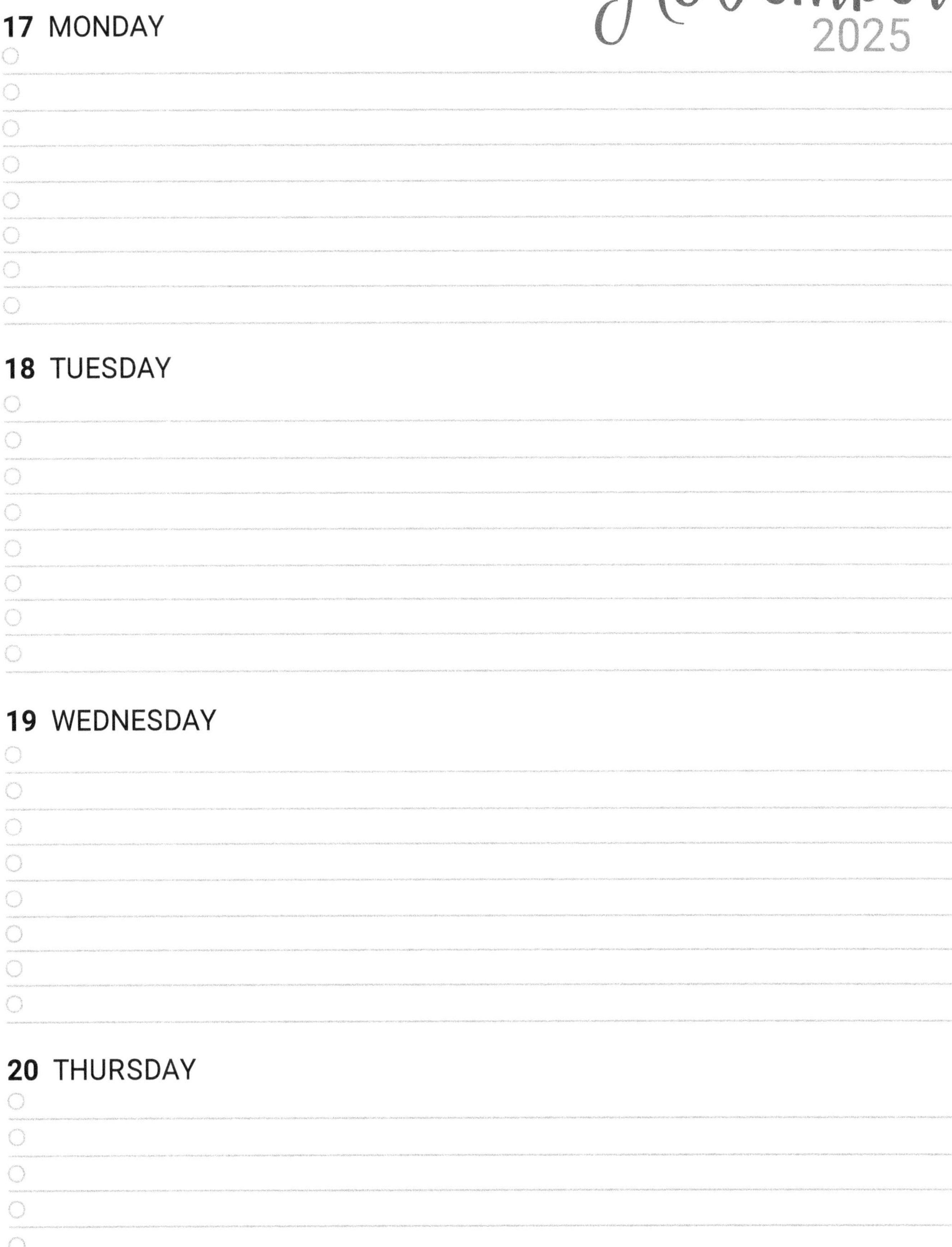

# November
## 2025

**17** MONDAY

**18** TUESDAY

**19** WEDNESDAY

**20** THURSDAY

**21** FRIDAY

**22** SATURDAY

**23** SUNDAY

**24** MONDAY

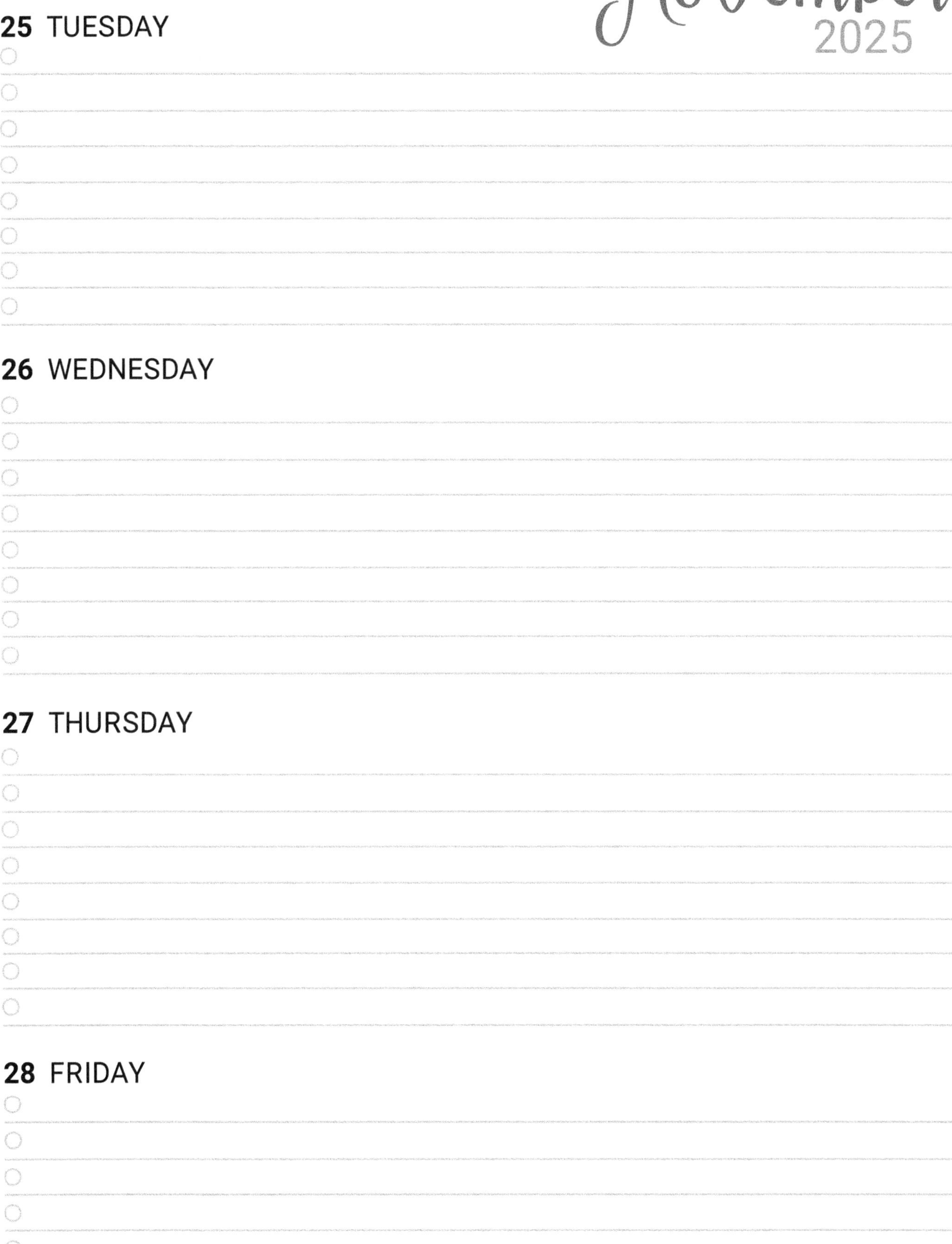



**25** TUESDAY

**26** WEDNESDAY

**27** THURSDAY

**28** FRIDAY

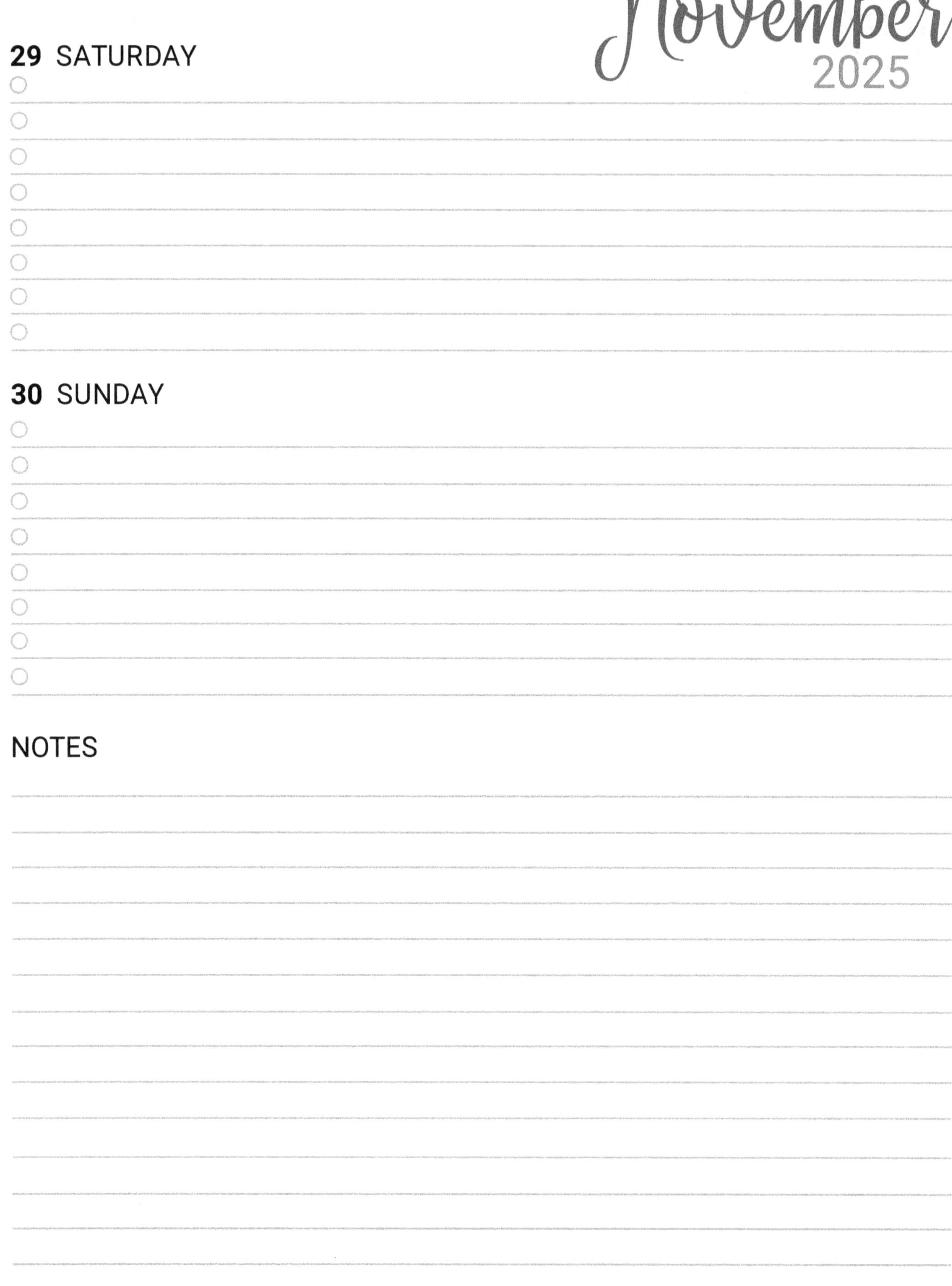



**29** SATURDAY

**30** SUNDAY

NOTES

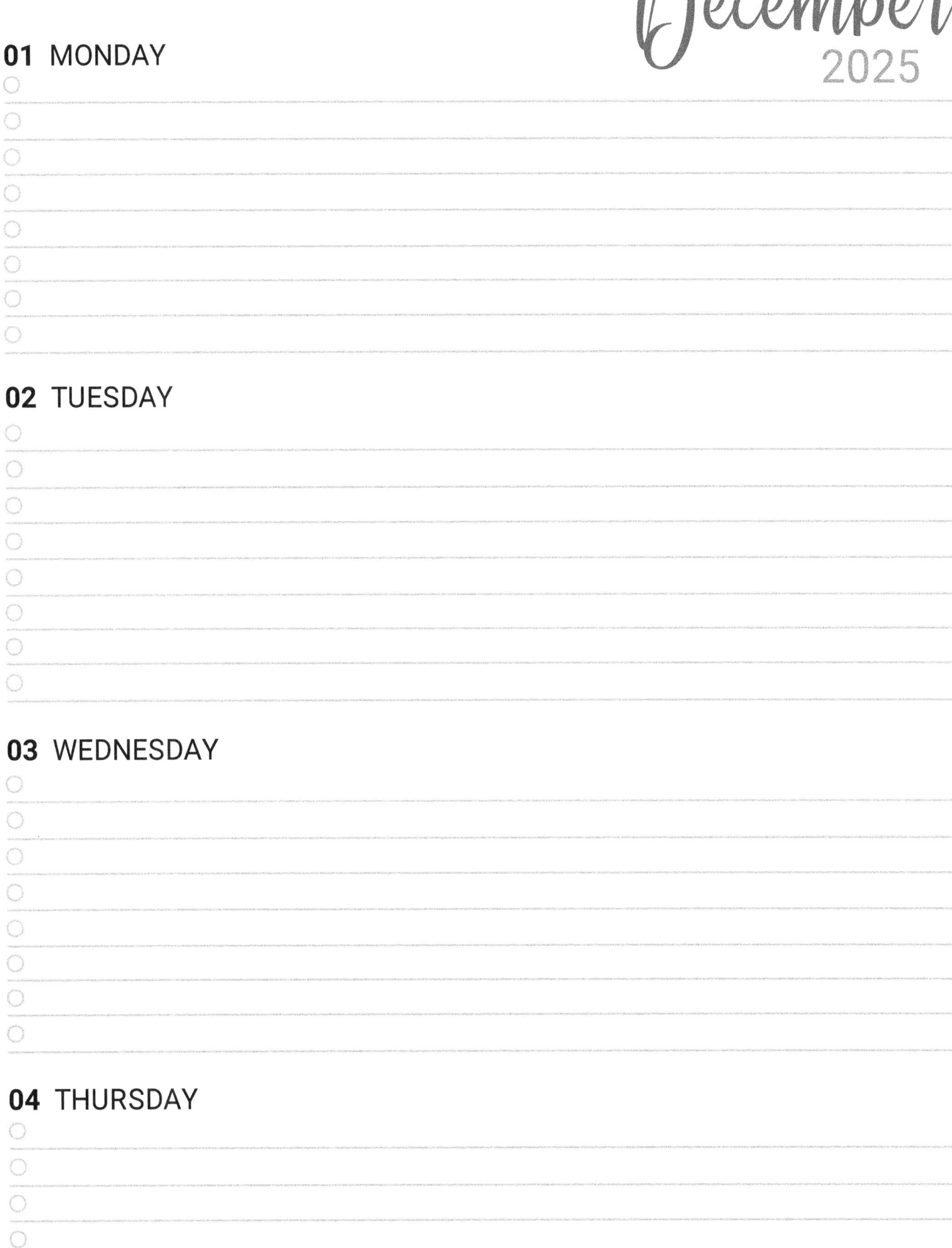

# December
## 2025

**01** MONDAY

**02** TUESDAY

**03** WEDNESDAY

**04** THURSDAY

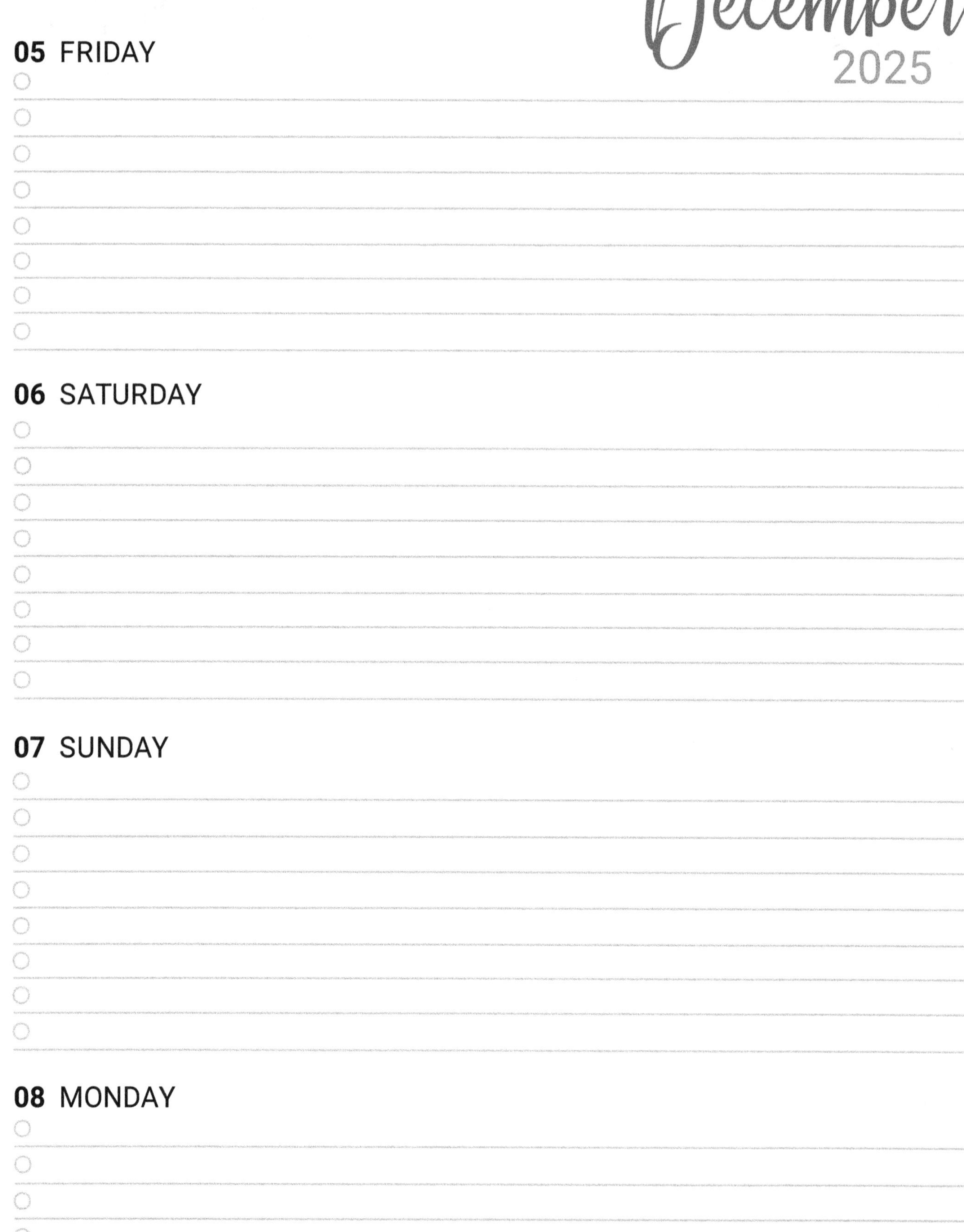



**05** FRIDAY

**06** SATURDAY

**07** SUNDAY

**08** MONDAY

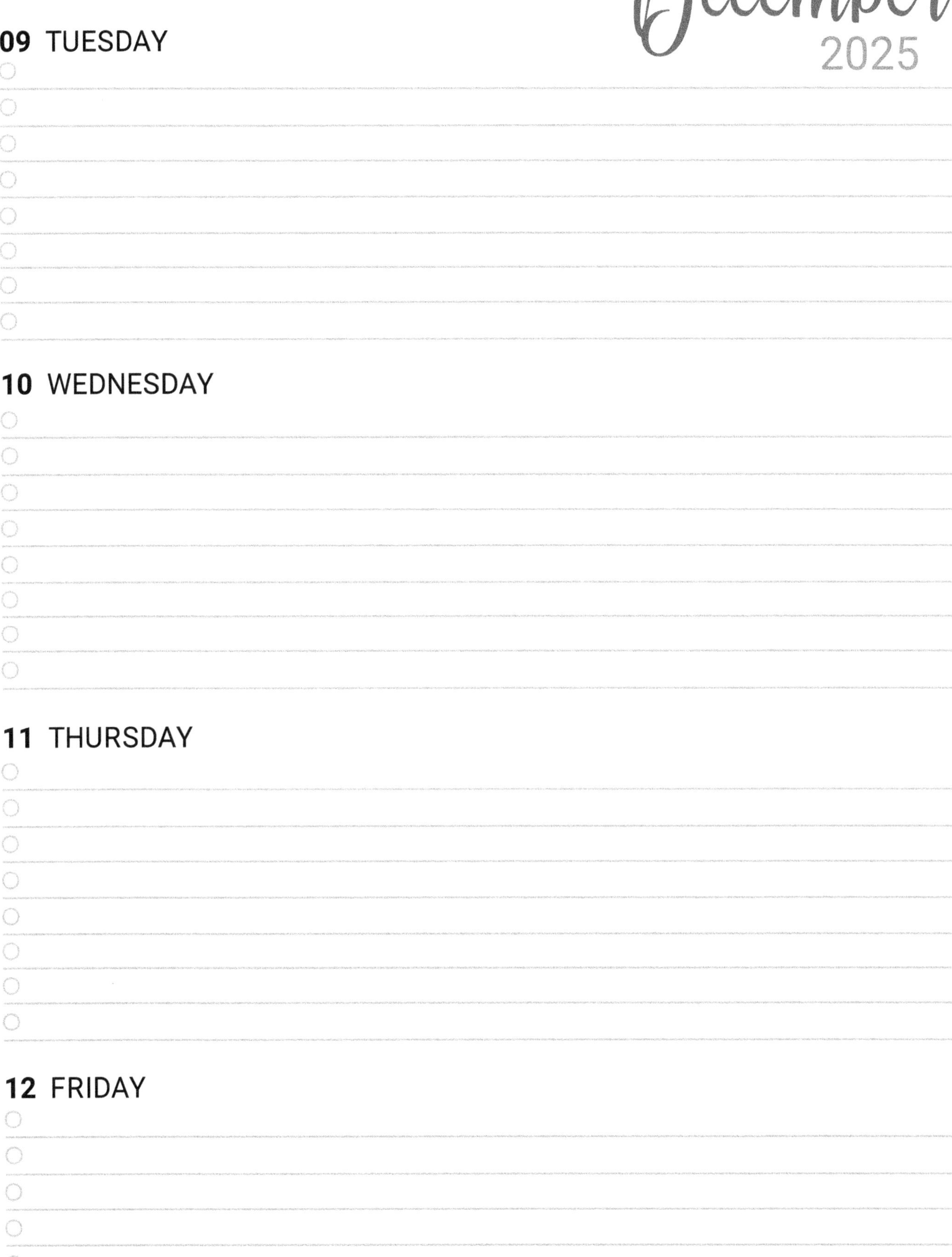



**09** TUESDAY

**10** WEDNESDAY

**11** THURSDAY

**12** FRIDAY

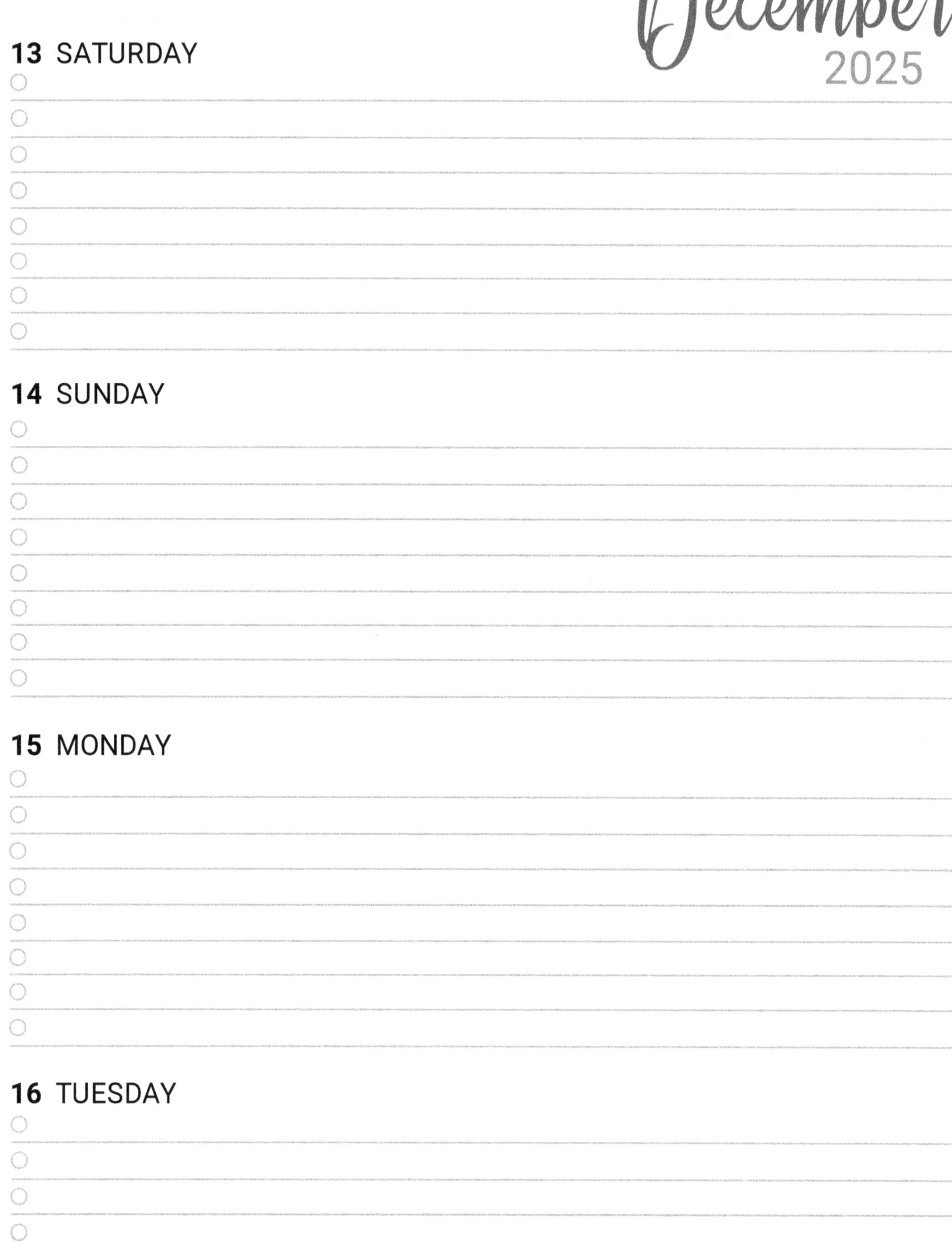



**13** SATURDAY

**14** SUNDAY

**15** MONDAY

**16** TUESDAY

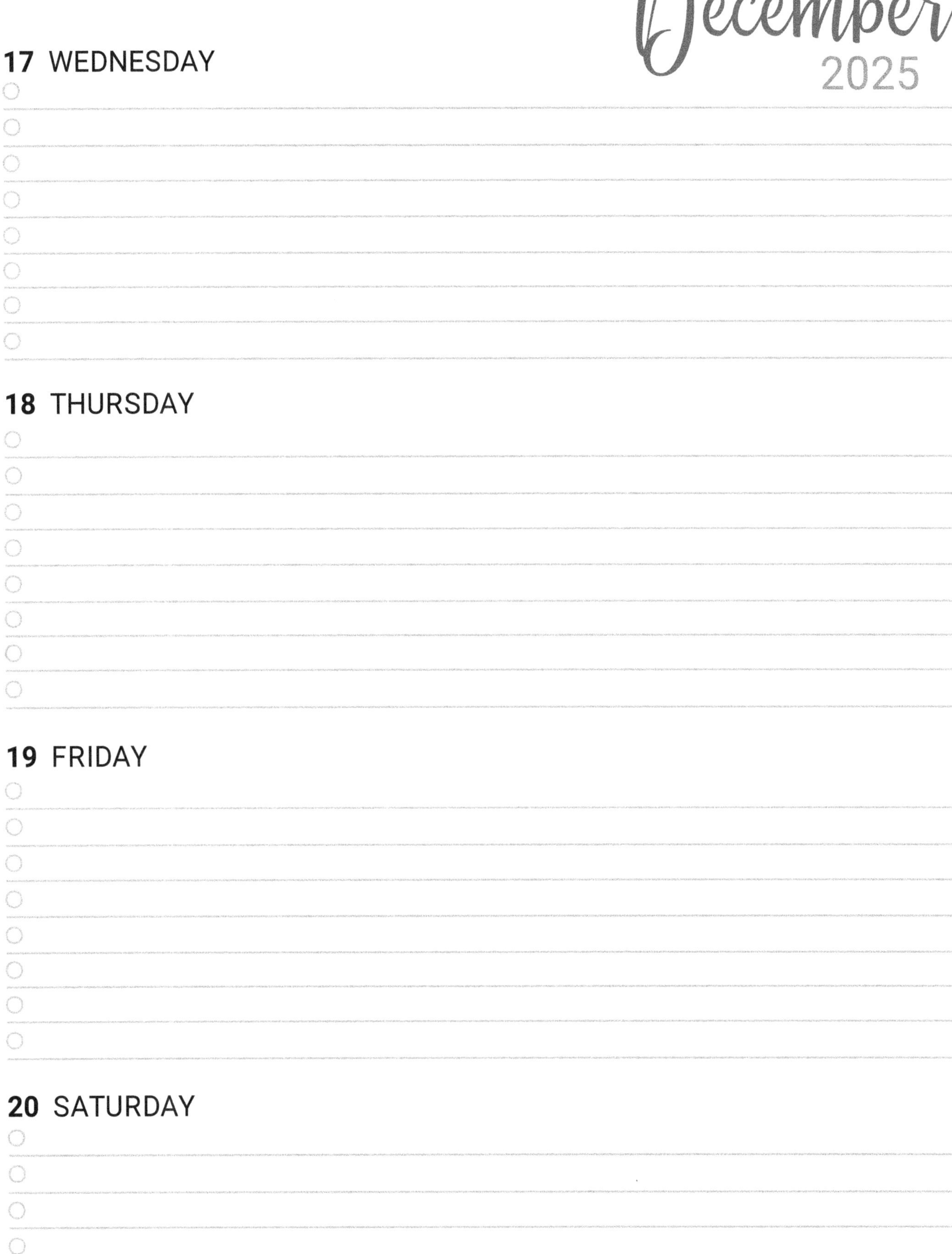



**17** WEDNESDAY

**18** THURSDAY

**19** FRIDAY

**20** SATURDAY

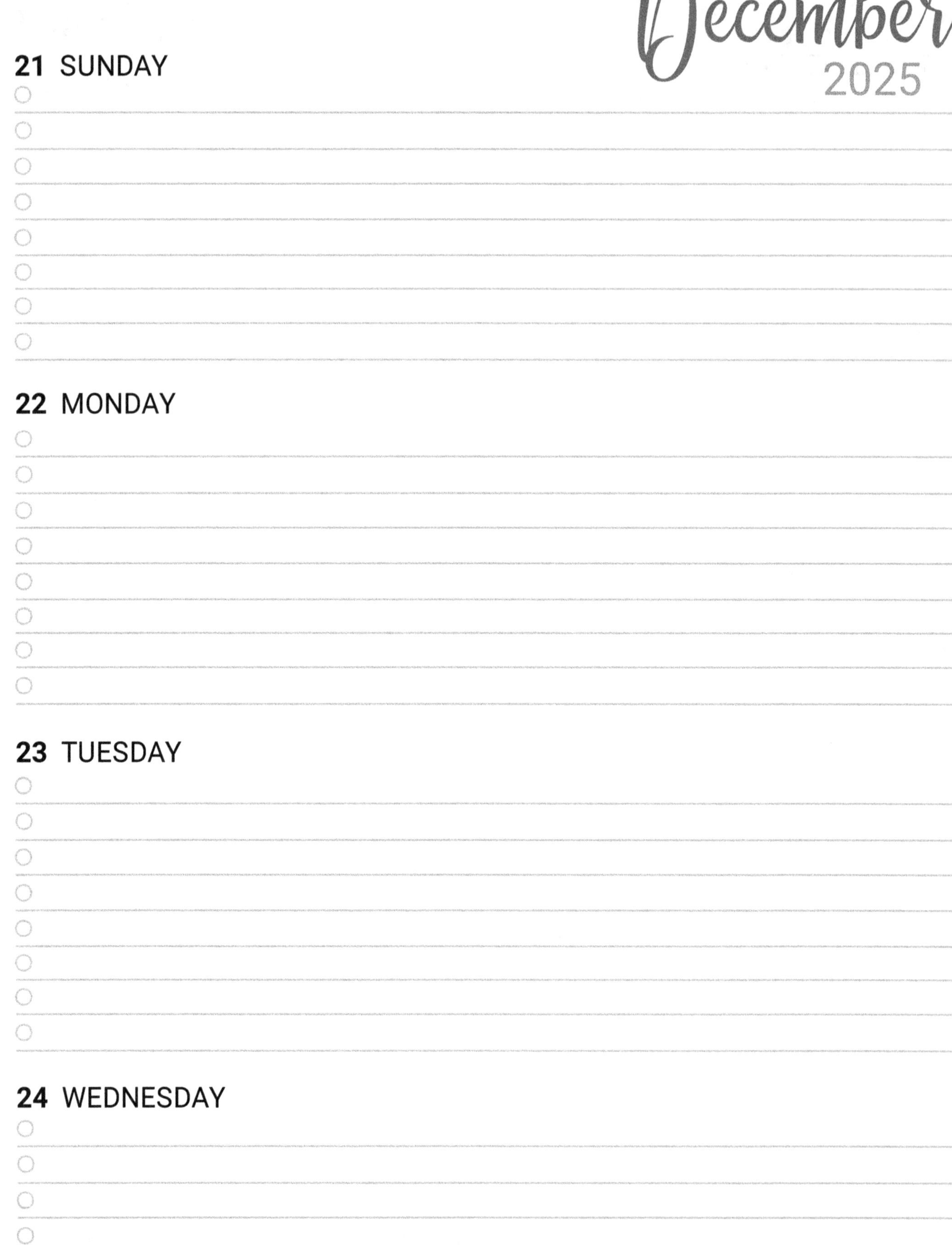

# December
## 2025

**21** SUNDAY

**22** MONDAY

**23** TUESDAY

**24** WEDNESDAY

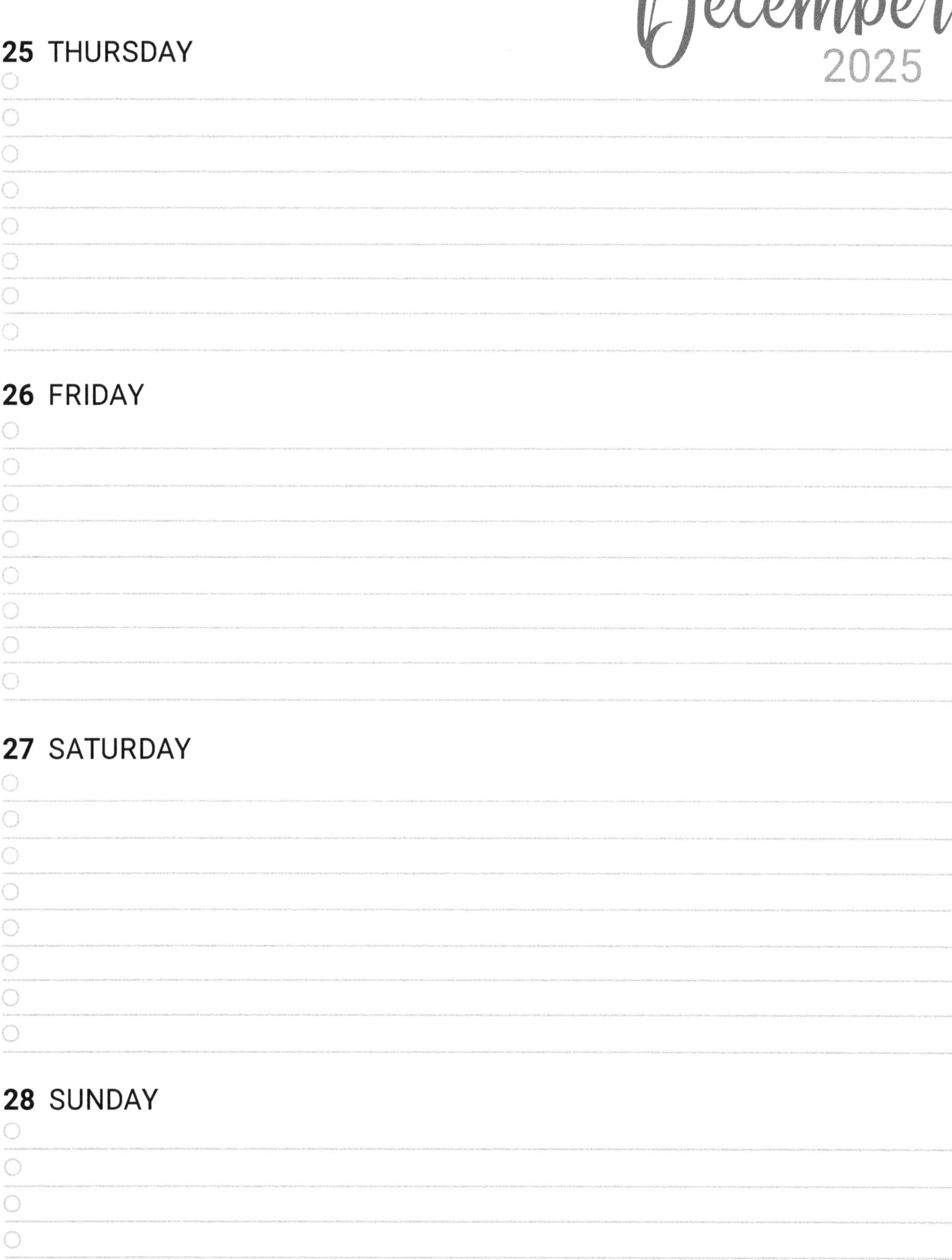



**25** THURSDAY

**26** FRIDAY

**27** SATURDAY

**28** SUNDAY

**29** MONDAY

**30** TUESDAY

**31** WEDNESDAY

NOTES

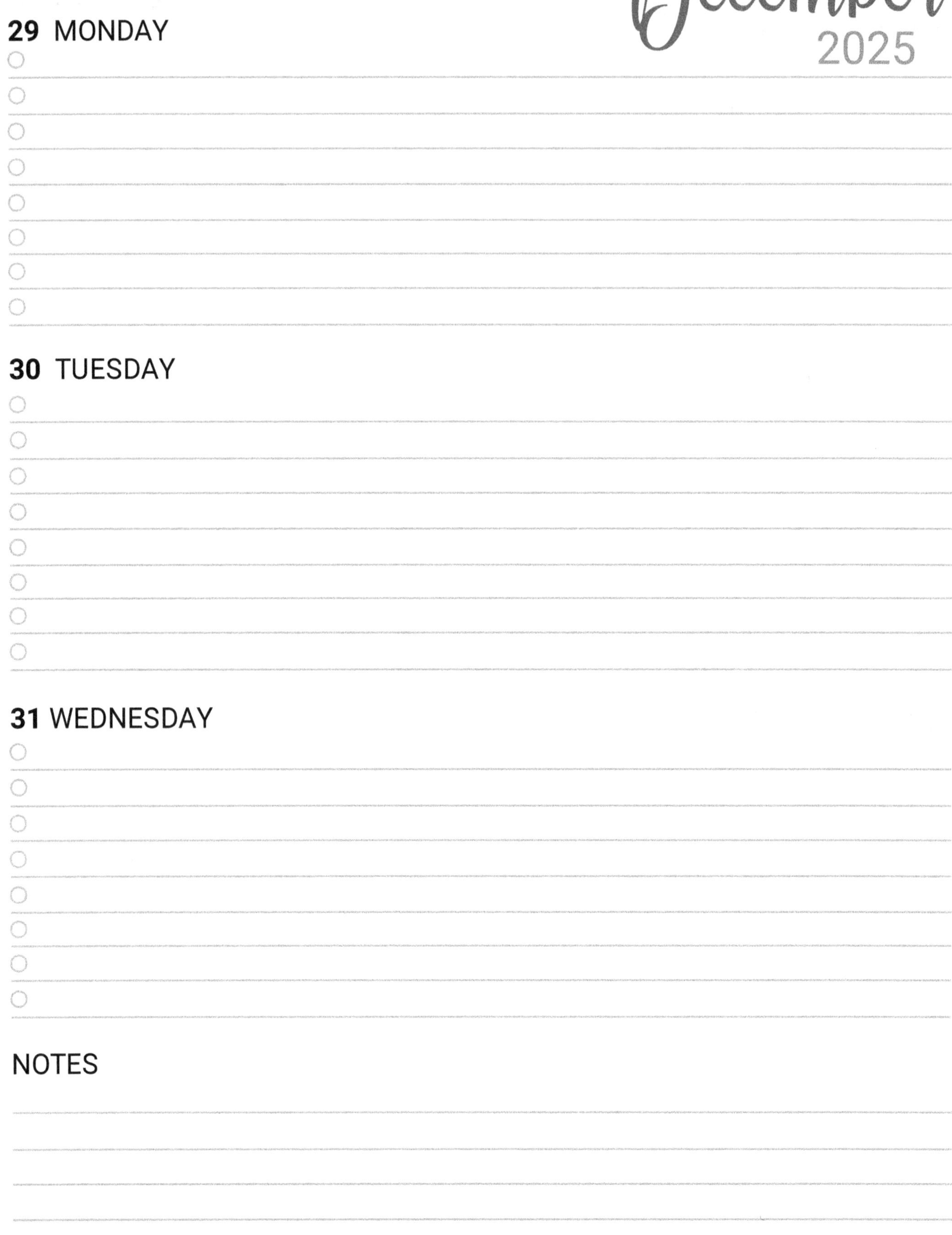